SHINE

SHINE

Winning at Work

Shirley Peddy PhD

Copyright © 2017 Shirley Peddy PhD
All rights reserved.

ISBN-13: 9781544183435
ISBN-10: 1544183437

*To those who want their time at work to mean something,
to those who are committed to improving themselves in the process,
to those who want to make a contribution to
something greater than their self-interest,
in other words, to those who want to SHINE,
this book is dedicated.*

Acknowledgments

The original book *Secrets of the Jungle* was written in 1996 shortly after I took an early retirement from one of the world's largest organizations. Today, the world of work has changed enough that I felt it time to acknowledge those differences and address new attitudes that have emerged. *Shine*, like *Secrets*, acknowledges the age-old truths that can be found in the jungle story, but it recognizes some important differences from the previous book as well. There are key additions to the insights and new ways of addressing the challenges of work today.

None of us live in isolation. Many of the key insights in *Shine* come from those people who played a major role in my work life as well as in my personal development.

I am greatly indebted to George V. Sherman, Jr. His ideas and advice played a key role in my career and in my writing. To him I owe many of the insights and secrets in this book.

I have been very fortunate in my career in having the opportunity to work with successful and wise colleagues. I am enriched from having known and worked with them.

The real-life experiences and stories of friends and family members who are still hard at work or have recently retired have contributed immeasurably to the examples in this book. Thank you so much for sharing them.

Contents

Acknowledgments · · · · · · · · · · · · · · · · · · · vii
To the Reader · xi

The First Secret:	On Learning, Mentors, and Tests · · · · · · · 1
The Second Secret:	On Feedback and Attitude · · · · · · · · · · · · 11
The Third Secret:	On Making Career Decisions · · · · · · · · · · 24
The Fourth Secret:	On People You Work With · · · · · · · · · · · 33
The Fifth Secret:	On Choices, Pitfalls, and Traps · · · · · · · · 45
The Sixth Secret:	On Perspective · 56
The Seventh Secret:	On Perception and Meaning · · · · · · · · · · 62
The Eighth Secret:	On Character and Reputation · · · · · · · · · 68
The Ninth Secret:	On Getting Your Work Approved · · · · · · 74
The Tenth Secret:	On Major Changes and Upheavals · · · · · · 85
The Eleventh Secret:	On Community · 96
The Twelfth Secret:	On Discovering Your Purpose · · · · · · · · 113

Epilogue: On Becoming a Mentor · · · · · 129
References · 137
Other Books by Shirley Peddy · · · · · · · · 139
The Author · 143

To the Reader

There are people who are *in* and people who are *out* in every organization; only the people who are *out* don't have a clue what the people who are *in* know. If you are *in*, opportunities to succeed and to enjoy your life at work abound. If you are *out*, living is something you do only after the work day ends. If you want to learn how to be *in* -- in other words, how to SHINE--this book is your mentoring guide.

Shine: Winning at Work©
Prologue

"Come to the edge," he said.
They said, "We are afraid."
"Come to the edge," he said.
They came.
He pushed them...
And they flew.

---Guillaume Apollinaire

THE DIFFERENCE BETWEEN TORCHES AND LAMPS
Two friends worked for the same company. Both had MBAs and both were intelligent and ambitious. Jack Sullivan had worked for Perry

Winkle Enterprises (PWE) for eighteen years. Rachel Hanson had been there for four. Although they were in different roles, they even reported to the same manager, Bill Jamieson. But there the similarity ended. In fact, if you talked to Jack or Rachel, you might think they worked for different companies. Jack was happy at PWE. People at every level and from all over the company sought his advice, asked for his help, and included him in their most important projects. They considered Jack a key member of the team.

Rachel was unhappy. She worked hard, but she did not feel appreciated. In fact, she was so busy working that she didn't have time to get involved in the work others were doing, and people realized that. They thought of Rachel as hard-working, dependable, and prompt, but they never thought of her when they wanted advice or help with something important. That was because most people saw her more as an individual contributor than a member of the team.

Late one Friday afternoon, she stopped by Jack's office. "I came to say goodbye, Jack. I am on my way to put this letter on Bill's desk. It's my resignation, dated tomorrow. Before I go, I wonder if you would mind if I asked you something. I know you must be getting ready to leave – but...."

"Of course I wouldn't mind," said Jack, his voice full of concern. He had played a part in recruiting Rachel, and he was disappointed that she was thinking of leaving.

"You seem so happy here at PWE. Everyone notices the work you do. You do not ask for it, but you seem to get a lot of credit and appreciation. I don't understand what you do to get all this approval. You don't work harder than I do, you don't put in longer hours, yet everyone asks your opinion. Managers who do not even nod to me in the hall come to your office just to *kick things around*. I know I must have done something wrong, but I can't figure out what it is." Her eyes welled with tears.

"I'm sorry you've been unhappy," said Jack, passing Rachel a box of tissues. He paused for a moment as she dabbed her eyes, then continued, "I don't think you've done anything wrong. But if you set your sights on approval, perhaps you've been aiming at the wrong target. Management approval is elusive – and even if you hit the mark, it doesn't last very long. You asked me how I did it. Well here is my secret. Once I forgot about making an *impression* and set my sights on *making a difference*, everything began to fall into place.

"I know you're discouraged, Rachel," he continued, "but look at it this way – you have discovered what most people never learn: doing your job just isn't enough. I am not suggesting that you work harder, but that you approach work in another way. Let me illustrate with an analogy: in business, some people are torches and some are lamps. Both are sources of light, but the difference is important. Torches use their own fuel and burn out, while lamps are plugged into a continuously renewing energy source."

"Energy source?"

"Yes," said Jack. "This energy comes from your network, your contacts, your mentors and other relationships. See what I mean."

"I do," said Rachel. "Maybe I've been operating more like a torch than a lamp, but no one told me all of these things were important. I thought the most important thing was sitting at my desk and getting my work done. Now it's too late."

"It's never too late for someone with your gifts. You're a talented person," he said, "and you do work hard. That entitles you to a paycheck and the opportunity to continue working for PWE, but it won't earn you the other rewards you described. I'll answer your question no matter what you decide, but I have a proposal for you. Stay with PWE for the next six months, and I'll teach you the secrets I've learned over the years."

Coming from Jack, that opportunity was too good to pass up, so Rachel decided to stay, and with Jack as her mentor, she, too, became a lamp that shone throughout the company. This is Rachel's story... and possibly yours.

Jack had been intrigued by the jungle since college when, undecided about his future, he had taken a year off to see the world and spent the better part of it with a biologist friend in the tropical rain forests of the Amazon. The jungle had taught him many lessons. There were rules for survival and secrets for traveling it successfully. Over time, he had come to realize many of the same rules and secrets exist in organizations. He was writing a book about these universal truths and invited Rachel to read and comment on it. This is how she learned many of the rules and most of the secrets that changed her life.

The First Secret

On Learning, Mentors, and Tests

*"Learning is not attained by Chance.
It must be sought for with ardor
And attended to with diligence."*

ABIGAIL ADAMS

Chapter One of Jack's book, *Secrets of the Jungle*, began…

Keli Meets the Elder
The road was overgrown with foliage. I could not find the path. My foot caught in the tangled roots of a mangrove tree, and I stumbled. My elbow was skinned and bloody. I could taste panic rising in my throat. Suddenly I felt a warm, calloused hand on my arm, helping me up. That was my first meeting with the Elder. I looked into kind brown eyes.
  "Are you lost?" he asked, his voice gentle and concerned.
  I felt lost. Almost two years had passed since I left the city behind me and returned to the Korios tribe. Somehow, everything was different than I had imagined it would be. I was an outsider. When I asked my fellow tribesmen what was wrong, they told me not to worry – I would find my place. I knew better. When others spoke at the tribal meetings, the Chiefs would listen, but if I asked a question or made a suggestion, I could hear them shuffling

their feet, see them nodding to each other as if to confirm something they had said outside of my hearing. I didn't understand what was going on, but I was sure of one thing – I didn't fit in.

I was confused. I didn't know which way to turn or what to do. I had walked for hours that day searching for answers when I lost my way and fell. And so I told the Elder my story. He listened and asked me many questions. He understood my words, but more than that, he understood the anxiety and fear beneath them. After that we talked many times. And so, my life changed. He taught me about the jungle: how to understand it, how to survive in it, and how to honor the lessons it taught me. And he started with the first rule: "if you would know the secrets of the jungle, you must dedicate yourself to learning."

"Learning what?" I asked.

"…learning how to find the secrets and how to use them effectively for your good and the good of the tribe. In so doing, you will set out on a path that leads to contribution and you will earn the respect of the Chiefs. Then when you speak at the tribal meetings, all will pay attention."

"I have learned," I protested. "I spent many years in school. I want to practice what I know."

"Patience," he told me. "Never believe you know all there is to know about the jungle, for when you do, you will be prey to its hidden dangers. What do you know of the jungle terrain?"

"I have seen the lianas wrapped around giant trees climbing toward the sun and the pond rich with red-eyed frogs. I've stood in the darkness of the forest where there is no light, and I've seen the sun rise above the hill."

"And?" he asked, waiting for me to continue.

"I have heard my teachers speak of the black caimans that live in the rivers and eat the tree frogs – and waters alive with tall red and white birds with long necks – and flesh eating fish."

"Yes, my son," said the Elder, "what you have seen for yourself and learned from others is only the beginning of your education. In school, you proved your ability to learn. You were trained by people who studied and learned about jungles and passed this information on to you; but most have

never lived or worked in this jungle. Like me, and every guide you will ever have, their perspective is limited. What you have gained in school is the privilege to join the tribe and learn."

"The jungle is a living system," he continued. "It can be hostile; it can be indifferent; or it can be friendly; but whatever it is, it is a place of challenge — of danger and of opportunity. To survive in it, you *must* learn its secrets. Those who ignore the dangers will run into hostile tribes, ferocious animals, and unfriendly territory. Those who take the time to learn about it will be rewarded."

Rachel could see how business might be like the jungle with its surprises and challenges. She turned to Jack, "but what's the best way to learn these things?"

"In school, you learned by reading books, listening to lectures, and asking questions. From time to time you were tested to be sure you could repeat the information to the satisfaction of your teachers. In business there are also schools, but you will learn most from the informal system by paying attention to experienced people who know the secrets, working with others who are successful, listening to their stories, and profiting from both praise and criticism."

Jack looked at Rachel intently. "Remember this -- you are constantly being tested. To pass, you must earn the respect of the people you work with, and, at the same time, treat them with respect whether you think they have earned it or not. Some people fail the test because they don't produce results, but more fail because they don't understand the importance of building working relationships with others."

"I get along with my peers," Rachel said, a bit defensively. "And I think Bill likes me, even though he ignores me most of the time."

"That's a start, but getting along is not enough. You need to develop friendships and relationships that last over the course of your career if you want to learn the secrets of the organizational jungle. At school, you will find your teachers in the classroom or in their offices. In business, they are everywhere. They are not only the supervisor who assigns you work and the manager who needs a report but also the person who brings you the mail and the secretary who takes your calls when you are out. They include the people who ask for your help and those who have high expectations of you. Some you will like; some you won't. Problems come when you don't recognize the people around you as your teachers and the opportunities and challenges they bring as tests."

"If my teachers are everyone, why use an elder in the story?"

"This is a book about being successful in the world of work. In order to do that you must have someone who can whisper the *unspoken rules* and secrets to you. What is an elder, but a mentor wise in the ways of the jungle, a spokesperson, a teacher, a confidant, and guide. In my eighteen years of organizational life, I have been guided by many elders."

"Can't you learn these things by yourself?" asked Rachel. "I mean, aren't there successful people who have never had a mentor?"

"Probably. Some people learn the rules intuitively. Most people don't. Someone once gave me this analogy: you can learn to hit a golf ball by going to a driving range and hitting a thousand balls, or you can take lessons from the pros. Which do you think makes the most sense?"

Rachel laughed. "Or you can sit in your office and wonder how other people get such great scores. So, what kinds of things did the pros teach you?"

"Let me give you a couple of examples. Mary was a highly-respected manager. She taught me the importance of finishing what I start. Speaking about someone who continuously brought her problems, she shook her head. 'I don't need anyone to find problems for me. I can identify enough problems in a day to keep me busy for a year,' she said. 'What I'm looking for are solutions. If you have a problem and a solution, come see me.'"

"Does that mean you should never bring someone a problem unless you know the answer? Wouldn't that cause many problems to be swept under the carpet and prevent people from correcting what's wrong?"

"That's a good point, Rachel. No, I don't think Mary meant that you shouldn't alert others to problems. What I think she meant is, if you encounter a problem in your work, don't be too quick to hand it off. That makes you appear weak and powerless. Try to solve it first. At the very least, come up with some recommendations. Then be sure to tell the boss what steps you've already taken. She'll appreciate your efforts, believe me."

Jack continued, "Mary also told me a secret that is among the hardest to learn and most important to remember – not to confuse criticism of my work with criticism of me. I remember the occasion well. My supervisor had written a comment on a report I wrote, and I was convinced he was wrong. In fact, I regarded it as a personal attack and was very offended by it. Mary was sympathetic. 'Write him a note,' she offered, 'and clarify your position.' So I wrote the note and asked Mary what she thought of it. 'Let's take personalities out of it,' she said, and suggested one edit that I'll never forget. I had written the sentence, 'I'd like to point out why I disagree with you.' Mary crossed out the words *with you*. Then I read it over: 'I'd like to point out why I disagree.' It softened the tone. Mary agreed. 'If you want to get things resolved, center your attention on the problem, not on the person. You've probably heard the old saying, you can always disagree without being disagreeable.'"

"Was Mary your mentor?"

"Yes," said Jack, "one of them. That is the second rule of the jungle. Be guided by the wisdom of others until others seek you out to learn what you know."

"But who are these others, and why should they care about me?"

"In the book Keli asks the Elder the same question. Here's the passage. Read his answer and tell me what you think."

"*Look beyond position in the tribe and see others as people. In the jungle we know that everyone is connected to the earth – and to each other. I know another through the things he keeps around him, what he talks about in the tribal meetings, the actions he takes. Therefore, in your quest for knowledge, look for those whose wisdom can guide you. Then use your powers of observation to find the connection."*

Looking up from the manuscript, Rachel nodded. "So you look at the pictures in their offices or things they keep on their desks or listen to their casual conversation to see what you have in common. Is that what you mean?"

"That's it," said Jack. "It can be as simple as you both love dogs. Perhaps you've visited the same places or you know the same people. Maybe you have children in the same age group or you have similar hobbies. Once you find something you can talk about, whether it's business or social, it's easier to make a connection. I recall starting a conversation with one manager about a quotation he had hanging on his wall. It's that simple. Refine your powers of observation and be a good listener. That's the key."

"I guess it helps if you're a golfer or enjoy football."

"It might, but don't focus on that. I've known a lot of successful men and women who couldn't swing a club or a racket and preferred the symphony to football."

"I was once assigned a mentor," said Rachel. "That didn't last long. At first I spent our weekly ten minute scheduled meetings listening and nodding my head in agreement as he checked off items he was supposed to discuss with me. Then, there were the five minute Q and A sessions at the end of the meetings. In between meetings I struggled with what to ask him. Before long, the whole thing fizzled out. We just had nothing to talk about."

Closing his eyes, Jack reflected for a moment. "Assigned mentors can help, but mentoring is a relationship based on choice and built on liking, trust, and reciprocity."

"Reciprocity?"

"Yes, Rachel. In every successful relationship, there must be something in it for both people. That's why assigned relationships tend to be less satisfying, and as you put it, often fizzle out." Jack chuckled. "I like the way you put that. Mind if I borrow it for the book?"

"Be my guest," Rachel said, smiling. "That makes our relationship reciprocal. Right?"

"Right! But don't think you do not have a lot to offer a mentor. Being a good listener, giving honest feedback, providing information, even giving advice—there are all sorts of things you can do. In one role I was in, it was my responsibility to find speakers for communication events. You'd be surprised how many executives welcomed the opportunity to speak to an audience of attentive participants."

Rachel leaned forward in her chair. "So you decide who you want to mentor you. Then what?"

"You already know one way to start a mentoring relationship: ask for advice about something. Isn't that how you and I got together? There are other ways as well. Mary was a manager in the Controller's Department. We worked on a project together, and we just liked each other. Dean was my boss's boss. I used to drop by his office to say hello. When I changed jobs, I stopped by his office to say goodbye. He said, 'Stay in touch,' and I did just that. He turned out to be one of the best mentors I ever had.

"It sounds like you made it happen. I mean, do mentors ever find you?"

"Sure. It's like any other relationship. You just click with some people and...."

"I get it," said Rachel. "So that's how torches become lamps. "

"It's a start. One thing I've learned in business as in life—relationships count. Having people care about you can sustain you in rough times. Just remember, having a mentor is not a substitute for performance.

"Developing mentoring relationships takes time. In your first year or two what you really need is a strong and patient coach, someone who can help you learn the way things work. I call these 'the unspoken rules.'"

"Unspoken rules? Does PWE have them?"

Jack nodded. "Every group has them. Members in good standing understand them. Newcomers or those on the outside are rarely privy to them. They tend to learn them only when they make a mistake. We learn these rules from our first mentor if we're lucky. This can be a supervisor, a peer or almost anyone. I remember when I first came to PWE. I had worked somewhere else before, and it was like crossing the border into another country. What I needed most then was a teacher and a translator, someone who could introduce me to the customs and help me interpret the language. I was lucky. My first mentor was the person who hired me. I remember how I used to go into Carla's office, close the door and ask questions about what to call managers, when to copy someone in a higher position--and when not to, what to wear to a PWE off-site meeting and how to interpret behaviors that happened in a meeting I attended.

"After I had been there a while, I needed someone to clue me in. Who were the people I needed to know? What other resources should I develop? That person functioned more like a guide. Mary played the role and she gave me the feedback that helped me become a better listener," he chuckled, "and a whole lot less defensive.

"Later, my mentor was more a supporter, a friend--someone I could laugh with, confide in and who shared my interests. Dean sponsored me in major projects. He knew the players and the game. When I needed funds that hadn't been budgeted, he knew how to find the money. When he retired, I felt the loss along with others he had mentored.

"I had several other mentors. They were sources of valuable information. Many times I learned about changes the company was planning like a downsizing or reorganization before they were announced."

"How come people were willing to tell you?"

"Because they trusted me and because I always followed certain rules."

"And you learned these rules--"

"From peers, from my personal values, and from observation. I just understood that most people want to be helpful if they are not harmed in the process. It takes a long time to establish trust and a very short time to destroy it. The rules are universal, and they make sense. People will tell you things if you follow them. Violate them and it's all over."

"So tell me, what are they?'

"I was just listing them to include in *Secrets*," said Jack reaching into his pocket. Rachel unfolded the paper and read what he had written:

- Build trust by being honest about your motives.
- Never break a confidence or tell anyone the source of your information.
- Never use another person to your advantage, for even in mentoring relationships, we are tested to see if we are worthy.

"I like your list," said Rachel, "but I'm not sure I understand what you mean by 'being tested'.'"

"Let me give you an example. I remember one time when I was on a project team with another employee. Let's call him Joe. Anyway, I was sure I was doing more than my share, and I was worried that I would be blamed if the project was late. My supervisor suggested I tell Joe's boss. I wasn't sure that was a good idea, so I went to Mary. I was exasperated and I told her that Joe was not a team player, and I felt he was taking advantage of me. Mary's facial expression stopped me in the middle of my rant. 'I wonder if you know Joe has a sick child at home,' she said. 'I know Joe, and I'm sure he would want to know your concerns. He's a good person, Jack. So are you. If you have a problem working together, the best way to handle that is with him...privately.'

"And that's what I did," continued Jack. "But I almost failed the test. Just think--what might have happened to our future relationship if I had taken my supervisor's advice. I also learned a very important secret from that encounter."

Rachel nodded. "Never put another person down. Right?"

"Right. And after that I was more thoughtful about what I said about another person. But I have seen others put down in meetings countless times. Once I even saw two people do this in a group meeting in front of top management. They soundly criticized one of their colleagues who wasn't even present to defend herself."

"Someone once told me feedback says as much about the giver as it does about the receiver," said Rachel.

Jack nodded. "Sometimes it says more. I know the behavior reflected badly on the people doing the talking. To me, it violated every rule of professional conduct I could name. Talk about failing the test!"

That evening Rachel started a journal to capture the key ideas she had learned from Jack.

JOURNAL ENTRY ONE
To Survive: Recognize the tests and the teachers.

To Succeed: Remember to use the rules of professional conduct in all your interactions.

To Shine: Find and develop the right mentor to teach you how to succeed in the jungle.

The Second Secret

On Feedback and Attitude

*"Change the way you look at things
and the things you look at change."*

WAYNE W. DYER

"Jack, can I see you right away?" It was Rachel on the phone and she sounded shaky.

"I've got a one o'clock meeting. It shouldn't take more than an hour. Can I call you then?"

"An audible sigh. "Okay."

It couldn't wait. Jack knew that instinctively. "Want to grab a bite of lunch with me? It's got to be in the cafeteria, but we could find a quiet table. You don't have much time to decide. I'm leaving right now."

He could hear the relief in her voice. "See you there. And, Jack, thanks."

She was sitting at a table in the corner with only a glass of water and an apple in front of her.

"Is that your normal lunch?" he asked, setting his tray down across from her. "Keep this up and you'll blow away before I finish the book."

"I just couldn't eat now, Jack. The apple is for later."

What's on your mind?"

"I just had a performance review with Bill. It was awful. I don't know if I should pack my bags now or not."

"Please don't. It's only been two weeks since you read Chapter One. Do you want to tell me what he said?"

"He basically sees me as average." She spat out the word as if it were poison. "Average! After all my long hours and hard work. I felt like crying -- or throwing his desk at him. He says I understand my job and do it well. Doesn't that count for anything? He says I don't have the big picture. We had quite a disagreement about that. I guess I reacted strongly, but I was shocked by what he said. Anyway, at the end of it, he told me I need to *lighten up*."

"Don't pack your bags. Average is not what you are, but clearly, it's Bill's perception of you. Anyway, since you didn't cry or throw the desk at him, you can put that in the win column. Look, Rachel, you're angry, and you need time to think about this. I'd like to give you the next piece of the book. It touches on feedback. Perhaps it will help. Then, when you've read it, we could get back together and strategize a bit. Deal?"

"Right now I'm willing to try anything that will help."

"One more thing, Rachel. Don't think this is the end of the world. Early in my career I had a similar episode with a supervisor. He saw me as 'creative but undisciplined.' He felt that I let things slip if I didn't find them important. He used the term: *unfocused* and a few others that escape me. My first reaction was just like yours. I wanted to leap over the desk and -- my career was over. I thought of quitting. I talked with Carla about it. You remember her. She's the person who coached me when I first came to PWE. She told me a similar story about feedback that a manager gave her. Then she added, 'the funny thing about it was, when I calmed down and thought about it, I could see some truth in what he said. I didn't like to hear it, and I particularly didn't like that way he said it, but he had a point.' The most important thing,' she said, 'is not to attack the messenger because then, the messages stop, or they get couched in such ambiguous language that the truth goes right over your head.'"

"So that's why you say it's a good thing I didn't throw the desk at Bill."

Jack laughed. "Somehow the image of your picking up the desk...."

"Okay, I get it, "Rachel said, responding with a weak smile.

Seeing a slight positive change in her demeanor, Jack smiled back. "There. That's more like you." Then he looked at his watch. "Gotta run. Will you come by at two or would you rather I brought the chapter to your office?"

"I'd rather come by yours. Right now, I'm not much in the mood to stay in my office. I've still got a few minutes. I think I'll take a couple of laps around the building."

When Rachel left work that night she had Chapter Two in hand. With Paul on a business trip, it would be a quiet evening, a good time for reading.

The Spirit of Learning

My first meeting with the Elder had given me a lot to think about. In his quiet and gentle way he had let me know that I had much to learn. But where should I start? I wanted to belong more than anything, to feel accepted by the tribe. I felt the need to talk to him. When I went to his house, I was disappointed at his absence. Someone told me he was sitting by the river. I found him there cutting into the brown roots of the cassava with a strange-looking knife.

"What is that?" I asked.

"It is a gift from Lutar, the toolmaker. He made it from the jaw of a peccary, a water pig. I shall now have no problem peeling the fruit." He offered me some of the root and we ate in silence.

"You are troubled," he said.

"How did you know?"

"It is written in your eyes, in the downturn of your mouth. How would I not know?"

"I am unhappy. Nothing is working out."

"Begin with all you search for."

"I want to belong, to be accepted. I want to feel useful. I want to be part of the laughter, not the one others laugh at. I want toolmakers like Lutar to carve a knife and give it to me as a gift, and I want to walk inside any hut and be as welcome as you are."

"That is a good list. You shall have all that and more. Now tell me, my son, what have you given?"

I shook my head. "Father, I have nothing to give. That is the problem."

"But you are of value," he replied. "Give of yourself."

"I don't understand."

"Start by adopting a spirit of learning. That is a commitment to be worthy of all you seek."

"But how will that help me. No one but you will know."

"Nor should they, for then you would be describing a wish. Commitment is best revealed by actions. You must be willing to be helpful without gratitude, eager to volunteer without reward, and able to accept criticism without anger. All of these acts will be noticed."

"But, what will I gain?"

"More than you give. Keli, why did you return to the Korios?"

"I was born a Korio. My mother left the tribe and went to the city to support me after my father died. She always kept our customs and told me many stories about the tribe. I never felt at home in the city. From the beginning, I knew I would return to the village someday to live with my people. Now, even after two years, I do not feel as if I belong."

"Keli you are a member of the tribe, but you are seen as uncommitted. You do not go out of your way for others. You walk into the jungle alone. You do not ask for what you need."

I hung my head. "I cannot hear this," I said.

He reached out and touched my shoulder. "My son, if you cannot hear this, I cannot help you."

I looked up. There were tears in his eyes. I was overwhelmed.

"Today there is a meeting. We will be choosing some people to help plan a celebration for the Chief's birthday. Shall I tell them you have volunteered to help?'

"Please," I responded eagerly. "I will take any job, no matter how small."
"It is done."

Rachel looked up from the book. She had taken a short break and was enjoying the second chapter. Jack was standing in the doorway to her office. "Sorry I didn't call. I was in the neighborhood. Feel like being interrupted?"

"I do. And before you ask, yes, I'm feeling better."

"Good. So, what did you think of Chapter Two?"

"I haven't finished it yet, but what I did read gave me some things to think about. There were two parts that really struck me. One was when the Elder told Keli, if you cannot accept feedback, I can't help you. I guess that's one of the areas I need to work on, big time."

"Don't feel bad about it, Rachel. Most people aren't good at giving feedback and few of us have enough self-esteem to be open to it, especially when it is delivered imperfectly, which it usually is. It helps to think of yourself as a business and feedback as information. You're Rachel, Inc., a company that wants to increase profitability, so you periodically survey your customers to see how the business is doing. Research shows that most customers of a business don't complain, even though they may be dissatisfied. They just switch to another supplier. Those who do complain or criticize often become its most loyal advocates. So it's to Rachel, Inc.'s, benefit to understand how her customers see her so she can increase her profits. Bill Jameson is your chief customer and he has given you his perspective. He says you are 'average.' That part is not too helpful. But he has told you a couple of specific things. He thinks you 'don't understand the big picture,' for one. The other is to 'lighten up.' Let's start with the first one. Okay?"

"Suits me."

"What's your guess as to why he thinks you don't understand the big picture?"

"I don't need to guess, Jack. He told me I don't get out of my office and meet people. He said I'm so wrapped up in what I'm doing that I don't seem available for other projects. He reminded me that when he was looking for a volunteer for the blood drive, I was polite, but disinterested. I told him I had been hard at work on a project he gave me with a short deadline, but he brushed that off as if it were unimportant. He said there had been other opportunities to volunteer, but I never did. I'm feeling very undervalued, Jack. Doesn't getting your work in on time count for anything?"

"Of course, it does. It sounds to me like Bill should have discussed this with you sooner--much sooner -- but that has no relevance to our point. How much of what Bill says fits?"

She hesitated, took a deep breath and blurted out, "All of it. I guess that's why I'm so angry. Why did he wait until my review?"

"Let's agree--he should have told you. But now he has, and that's the important thing to Rachel, Inc. Bill's a good guy. He may be stating his own opinion, or he may be reflecting things he has heard from others. Now you know what's on his mind you can come up with a plan that takes you out of the office and into the middle of what's going on."

"I can do that. My problem is, I'm having trouble understanding what the fuss is about."

"It's about commitment, Rachel. And it's vitally important. Let me explain. There are five levels of commitment at work. At the lowest level are the people who come to work every day, put in their eight hours and go home. For some, that's what a job is--a place to go to earn money to support themselves and their families. No more, no less. Their commitment is to their paychecks--and the company realizes that. It gets a fair amount of work from them, but the level of commitment is mutually low.

"Then there are the people who are committed to the job as the means to an end. That's the next level. This can take several directions--as a stepping stone to personal growth, or as a means to advance their own agenda. Those who use it for their own growth usually don't plan to stay. They see their present job as an interim move toward what they really want. Those who work their own agenda focus only on what makes them look good. If they can hand their work over to another or fail to do it, it's okay as long as the boss doesn't find out. If you ever inherit a job from one of those folks, you wind up with a mess of things that have fallen through cracks. In either case, the commitment is to self and as far as the organization is concerned, it tends to be short term."

"I've known a couple of people like that," Rachel said, nodding. "They are eager to get your help but reluctant to give theirs. In time, everyone catches on."

"Right. Now the third level is made up of people committed to their professions. They provide the company an excellent service. When the organization no longer satisfies their needs or *vice versa*, they move on. The commitment on both sides is a business transaction, a *quid pro quo*.

"The fourth level is people who are committed to the work or the work product. You give them a job and they do it, and they ask for more. They don't get around too much because they are too busy doing the work of several people. The organization may appreciate their work but often overlooks their sacrifices and personal contributions when it comes to handing out rewards. It's a narrow view, I admit, and I'm not saying it's fair, but I've heard such people referred to as 'workhorses.'"

"Workhorses! Tell me the truth, Jack. Is that how Bill sees me?"

"After you've heard the description of all five levels, you can tell me where you see yourself and where you want to be. Okay?"

"Okay, but I think I'm getting sick to my stomach."

"You're fine and I'm oversimplifying. None of what I'm describing is fatal, and it needn't be permanent. Now the fifth level is made up of those who link their own success to the prosperity of the company. Because they are committed, they focus their skills and abilities on what the organization is trying to achieve. They have a broad perspective on how and why the business operates the way it does, and they don't adopt an adversarial point of view. That attitude enables them to make more effective contributions. They refer to the organization as "us" not as "them." Companies usually put the highest value on this level of commitment.

"What you're saying is, so much of how we're seen is based on our attitude."

"Exactly. Our attitudes show up in our behavior. In the end, that affects the way the company views us and the way it rewards us."

"Okay. I'm in the workhorse group. Right?"

"What do you think?"

"I don't like it, but it's pretty accurate. So how do I break out of it and move to the fifth level?"

"Bill has given you some hints. The plan you devise should take them into account. Volunteer for something that PWE values, but be sure it gets you out of your office. There are always projects and task forces coming up."

"Yes, and I think Bill's looking for someone to coordinate the United Way Drive for our group. I'm the woman for that. I always donate anyway, and I believe it's worthwhile."

"That's a start, Rachel. You need to get out and around. Create opportunities for personal contacts with people--the sooner, the better. Read the annual and quarterly reports from cover to cover. Go to meetings. Get acquainted with people who've been around for a while. Ask good questions and make notes of the answers. Oh, and make sure Bill is aware of what you're doing."

"How do I fit all that in when I'm already bringing work home?"

"The secret is to create discretionary time."

"Discretionary time? I'm overbooked right now. How do you do it?"

"Rachel, it's all part of your transformation from a torch to a lamp. That includes not only how you do your work but also what work you do. Let's get back to Rachel, Inc. She has a role to perform--notice I didn't say a job. So, the first thing you need to do is clarify your role with Bill, one more time. Make sure your role contributes in even a small way to the 'big picture' as Bill sees it. Why does PWE have someone doing what you do? What value does the role have?

"Next, look at the work. Does all of it make sense given your role? Separate those items that contribute from those that merely use up time. You probably know the eighty-twenty rule."

"I heard about it in business school," said Rachel. "The idea is that a small amount of your work, for the sake of argument, roughly twenty percent, contributes most to your effectiveness. So should I find eighty percent to drop, Jack?"

Jack stifled a laugh. "Hmm. Perhaps a bit less. However, every job we inherit has leftovers created by someone else. Talk to your customers, those you interact with and those who use your work product. None of us works in a vacuum. For some people you are a supplier; for others, a customer. Those people can tell you what part of your work adds the most value and the least to their positions. Get them to tell you. That can be very convincing information in talking with Bill. And don't forget to ask for some personal feedback from them as well. It's all good information for Rachel, Inc. With that in mind create your list of priorities."

"Okay, I get it. I'm going to develop a plan--and run it by Bill; that's after I've gone over it with you, if you're willing."

"Of course, I'm willing. Aren't you going to read every page of my book and talk it over with me? That's reciprocity, my friend. Now, you said there was a second piece in the story that had a special message for you. What was that?"

"It was when the Elder asked Keli what he wanted and what he had given to make that happen. Jack, I took a deep breath before reading on."

"Why is that?"

"Because I can see that I have been sitting in my office waiting for good things to happen. No wonder they haven't."

"But you're going to make them happen, Rachel. That's what it's all about. Let's talk about Bill's other comment, the one when he told you to lighten up. What was that about? You think it was a general comment or specific to the occasion?"

"Both, I think. He told me that I seem to require a lot of positive support and praise as if I constantly have my hand out. He says that when he gives me feedback about ways I can improve that I get defensive. I admit I can be oversensitive, but – is that the way I come across to you, Jack?"

"To be honest, it isn't. But what we are talking about is not fact but perception. It's the way Bill experiences you. The question is not who is right or wrong, but rather how you can change Bill's perception and let him see the Rachel I see. Let's talk about a plan."

"I think I need to meet with him, don't you?"

"I do. You need to get more information but don't walk into his office without a plan. Prepare a list. Make him a co-conspirator in your success and you're a shoo-in. Also that will help him see you as more willing to accept feedback. It's a good start at mending fences."

"So you don't think I'm hopeless."

Jack smiled. "Not completely," he said.

Rachel laughed. "Thanks a lot, Jack. You're a big help. Anyway, I'm going to work on my plan this afternoon, and I will read the rest of Chapter 2 tonight. If you're free for a few minutes after lunch tomorrow, I'd like to stop by and discuss both of them."

They agreed on 2 o'clock the following day. Paul had returned from the trip with work to do, and Brad, their ten year old son, was spending the night with his best friend, so Rachel curled up on the sofa and continued reading.

It was three days before I spoke more than a few words to the Elder. I had been busy due to his efforts on my behalf. True to his word, he had given my name to Bari, the Hunter, who was in charge of the celebration, and I was soon engaged in small tasks like gathering sticks of wood for the cooking fire and flowers to decorate the tribal chief's house. I'm not sure but I think

Shine

Bari was testing my resolve by assigning me these small tasks, for the next day he sent Pardo, the trader, to ask me to help plan the dancing. This was much more to my liking since it involved talking to villagers who had only nodded to me in passing before.

The night of the celebration, I sat watching the dancers perform. They had dances about almost every aspect of village life, some that told the history of the tribe, some that demonstrated the hunt, and still others that told about headhunters and tribal wars that had happened many years before.

Many of the villagers came and sat beside me for a few minutes that night to pass the time. Several of the older ones remembered my mother and were grieved to learn of her death. It was strange. I had been in the tribe two years, but this was the first time I had felt a part of it. There was a hand on my shoulder, a familiar calloused hand. "My young friend, many seek your company tonight."

Before I could jump up, he sat down cross-legged beside me. "Father, this has been the best three days since I came to the tribe. And I have you to thank for it."

"Not so, my son, for my part in it was very small," said the Elder. "Never forget, Keli, all good things lie in wait for those who would reach out to help others."

"You do like my plan, don't you, Jack?" asked Rachel, putting papers back in her briefcase.

"I do," he replied. "I think it addresses Bill's concerns and at the same time gets you started on your strategy to get out of the office, meet more people, and broaden your interests. I think Bill will be impressed with the thought you've given to your role. Once you both agree, things will start happening."

"Well, I'm going to acknowledge right up front that I need his advice and his help."

"Nice work, Rachel."

"The story--I like the way the chapter ended. I can identify with Keli, I mean when he doesn't ask for what he wants. Sometimes I don't either."

"Because....?"

"Because it feels so risky. It's much easier to stay in your shell."

"But when you stay in your shell, no one can help you, and you stand no chance of getting what you want. Quick story. Several years ago there was a shortage of computers at PWE. At the time, I was supervising a group of people writing press releases and news items. We added a person to the group and were short one computer. That meant people had to share. Then I learned of one that was sitting in a vacant office. I went to my supervisor, explained the situation, and asked for it. At first my supervisor resisted, but I explained that it was an important work tool for someone who would do a large amount of writing and revisions. He agreed and the computer was delivered.

"About a week later, Jerry Evans came to me and said, 'How did you get that computer? I had my eye on it.' 'I asked for it,' I replied. 'I understand it's been in that vacant office for at least six weeks.' "I know,' said Jerry, 'but I was waiting for Chris to come around and ask who needed it.' Now eventually Jerry got a computer, but I never felt bad for taking that one. That's one of the secrets of the jungle. If you want to get what you need, don't be afraid to ask."

"What if you are told no?"

"Rachel, one of the ways we can all lighten up, and I'll include myself in this, is to learn how to hear things we don't want to hear. That includes feedback, and it includes 'no.' Most of my supervisors were willing to explain why they turned me down, if they did. More often than not, I hadn't been completely clear about why I was making the request or how others would benefit. Many times I was able to win a concession to come back with more information and ask again later. The secret is the more we listen, the more we understand, and the more we understand, the stronger and more capable we become. Back in her office, a few minutes later, Rachel took out her journal and wrote:

JOURNAL ENTRY TWO

To Survive: Clarify your role by keeping in contact with your customers and suppliers.

To Succeed: Ask for what you need, including feedback on how you are perceived. Treat feedback as helpful information about the past delivered in the present.

To Shine: Think of yourself as a business--like Rachel, Inc. Plan for your own development, and share that plan with your supervisor.

The Third Secret

On Making Career Decisions

"Chance favors the prepared mind."

Louis Pasteur

It was several months later when Rachel came to Jack for advice. Things were going better for her at PWE. Through following Jack's advice, she had greatly improved Bill's opinion of her, and he was firmly on her team. Now she had been offered a transfer to Marketing, and she wasn't sure whether to take it.

"I don't know what to do," she said. "This is in sales and I've never done it before. I'm not sure I would like it.. And I don't know anything about the Marketing Department. Besides, I am doing so much better here -- thanks to you, my friend."

Jack smiled. "Thanks to your hard work, Rachel. What does Bill say?"

"He thinks I should take it. He told me he would hate to lose me, but he thinks it's a great opportunity and good for my career. Tell me what to do. I really trust your judgment."

" I'm happy for you," said Jack. "It's great to have choices. I'd be glad to help you explore yours, but you have to make the decision."

"But how?"

"Well, first you need to consider your career goals. How does this offer fit in?"

"Jack, I'm not even sure what you mean by the term *career goals*."

"A good definition is a start. One way to look at a career is as your continuous development toward a specific goal in your work life. Another way to look at it, which is less specific, is the progression of work experiences that enhance your value to your profession or the organization where you work."

"What happens if you're not sure of your goal?"

"Good question. Let's get back to the Marketing offer. Since you are unsure of your specific goal, the second definition might offer more answers. What could you learn in Marketing that might increase your value and provide you more options in the future?"

"It might be a good way to get me out of my shell. It also might provide me with opportunities to build on what I already know about PWE's products."

"Right. There are probably more advantages if you put your mind to it. For example, you'll broaden your network. There's no question that networks are one of the most important keys to your success as a lamp rather than a torch. And speaking of careers, perhaps you could garner some more ideas by taking a look at what happens when Keli seeks the advice of the Elder as he searches for his own path."

" Somehow I knew this was coming," Rachel said smiling and holding out her hand. That night she read the next chapter in Jack's book.

The Four Paths
I was ready to explore the jungle, but which path should I take? I needed advice. I found the Elder as he was leaving a tribal council. We sat on a fallen tree limb by the edge of the pond.

"There are many paths through the jungle," he told me. "Tomorrow we will walk the path that leads to the tallest mountain."

We began our walk early the next morning. As we left the village, the Elder pointed out subtle changes in the terrain. Near the village was a quiet stream, but as we walked further toward the mountain, the current moved faster and faster. In areas where the river expanded, the dense growth of vines, shrubs, and small trees made walking more difficult.

We gathered berries as we walked along the path and stopped for lunch in a small clearing. "I never realized how much is required on the path to the mountain," I observed.

The Elder responded, "You must be totally committed if you choose this path. It is a hard path and requires many sacrifices. That is why many who start up this path change their minds along the way."

Reading this passage, Rachel nodded. From the standpoint of most employees, top management had it made. Few realized the sacrifices that were required or the level of responsibility involved. President Harry Truman had put it in perspective with a desk sign on which were the words, "The buck stops here." Great leaders share the credit for their achievements, but they also take the blame for their failures. Mediocre "leaders" blame everyone and everything else. Rachel paused to take a sip of hot tea and turned back to the chapter.

The next morning we headed down a more quiet path, away from the river's edge and toward a small hill. The trees in this area were smaller and closer together, but the path was more defined and easier to travel than the one we took the day before.

When we reached the top, the Elder used a small branch to draw four lines in the dirt. "These are the paths open to you." He pointed to one line. "This path goes through the wildest part of the jungle. It is the path of the Hunter. Of all members of the tribe, the Hunter is the most valued, for he brings home the tapir meat and peccary skins that enable the tribe to survive. If you take this path, you will go with others into places filled with jaguars and caimans, in forests where bushmasters lie in wait and rivers are filled with piranha. In our tribe, if you survive these dangers, you are likely to be chosen to take the path to the top of the tall mountain.

"The second path is that of the Toolmaker," he continued. This is the path of the craftsman. To follow it, you must learn to shape bows and carve arrows from the purple wood of the spotted snake wood tree and turn the

skins brought back by the Hunters into leather goods. If you would be successful as a Toolmaker, you must not only know your craft but also be constantly looking for ways to make better bows and finer leathers at the same time you reduce what must be thrown away."

Motioning me to turn in a new direction, the Elder pointed toward the river. "That is the path of the Trader," he said. I saw where the river forked away from the mountain and toward another part of the jungle. "The Trader must know the value of the leather and tools as well as the supplies we are trading for. He must have the skills to bargain with those who would hope to buy our products for too little and sell theirs for too much."

"It sounds like Traders have to think fast and be good talkers."

Rachel looked up from the page. "It sounds very much like Marketing," she thought.

"Yes," said the Elder. "To walk any path, you must use your intelligence and reasoning skills, but the Traders must use their minds and voices like the craftsman uses his tools."

"Do they climb the tall mountain?"

"Some do. Most set their sights on one of the higher hills, not as tall, but for them, just as challenging."

We turned once more and I saw a small group walking along a path carrying baskets full of foliage. "They are the Healers," said the Elder, pointing to the fourth line he had drawn. "Those roots, berries, and leaves they carry make medicines and balms with curative power. The Healers are knowledgeable about many areas that apply to people and the villagers depend on them for advice and counsel in every aspect of their lives."

"Do they ever climb the tall mountain?"

"No," replied the Elder, "but they are valuable counselors to those who do. There are other hills you can climb if you choose this path."

Just then I noticed another group of villagers. They did not appear to be in a hurry as they ambled from path to path. I was confused. "What are they doing?"

"They have not discovered their path yet," replied the Elder. "Some will seek help and be fine, while others will go from one path to another finding

little satisfaction since they have no goals. They are the Drifters. Many live their lives without purpose or commitment."

"I don't want to go down that path. I like the path of the Healer, even though it doesn't lead to the tall mountain."

"There is much satisfaction in being a Healer," the Elder said. "That is the path that I took as well." *Keli smiled with satisfaction.*

Rachel put the manuscript on Jack's desk. "I liked this part. It gave me something to think about. I don't want to climb to the top of the high mountain either, but I wouldn't mind the view from part way up. I think I'll talk to the Marketing Manager. If it sounds promising, I'll take the job. If I'm not happy there, I'll come back. I really enjoy this work."

"I don't want to leave you with the impression that you should 'try it out,'" Jack said. "There are many ways you can transform a job that you don't enjoy into one that you do. I remember one job in particular. It was one-third selling, one-third reporting, and one-third handling customer complaints. I enjoyed the selling, found the reporting dull, and disliked handling everyone's complaints. The first four months of that job I reduced the reporting by over half."

"How?"

"I examined the reports and determined how much each one cost PWE. I asked the ones who received the report how it was used. Remember, we talked about using this technique to find discretionary time. I found that some reports were filed but not used. Some were used partially, and some were used for making key decisions. Because I knew how much each cost, I had no arguments from anyone when I stopped doing those that weren't being used. I redesigned those that were partially used, in most cases combining them and making them shorter. In some cases I simply added the information to the reports that were used. By the way, Rachel, that's one of my best kept secrets. Always know what the work you do costs."

"How did you use your extra time? Did you handle more complaints? Or did you do more selling?"

"My second goal was to reduce the time I spent handling customer complaints. Let me be clear! I never minded handling my complaints. Complaints help us be more effective and I got larger sales and more loyalty from those customers who complained than from those who didn't. What I didn't like was handling everyone's complaints. That was always the work given to the newest employee."

Rachel rolled her eyes. "I sure hope they don't hand me that job in Marketing," she said. "How did you work that job?"

Jack smiled. "I had a plan. What I did was calculate the value of my customer complaints and showed the percentage of sales increases I had gotten from them to PWE's advantage. When I showed this to my manager, he asked me to make a presentation to the whole group. Once everyone had this information, there was a mob scene at my office with salespersons eager to retrieve the complaints belonging to them. It turned out to be a great sales tool, and my boss commended me for it. It was at this point that I learned another secret of the jungle. Along with knowing the cost of the work you do, it is important to know the value, in real money. Before long, I was spending about two-thirds of my time selling with one-third split between complaints and reports, and I really loved that job."

"Did you ever had a job you just hated?"

"I did have one that I didn't enjoy much. In fact, it was the one before my selling job. It was described to me as a coordinator's job, but I soon learned that it was shuffling lots of paper. The job was a series of activities and few of them were profitable. I was working with outside companies that were supposed to locate materials we needed. My phone rang all day long from outside sales people trying to sell their products, and I took my briefcase home every night bulging with paperwork."

"That sounds like the job from hell!"

"It was. I did reorganize it, and I put what I could on a computer. I also ran some surveys to see how we could improve the process. In the end, I plotted my escape."

"I must know how did you do it?"

"I took advantage of an opportunity. Mary had been on a committee to determine what kind of customer and supplier surveys were needed in their organization. The person in marketing who was the resident expert on surveys was transferred. Mary knew I had experience with surveys. Before long, I was an adviser to their committee. Soon after that Marketing arranged a transfer and I wound up in the sales job."

"Was Mary your supervisor?" asked Rachel.

"No," replied Jack. "I never worked for her -- just with her."

"Sounds like it was a combination of mentoring and opportunity that helped you make your escape from that awful job."

"It was more than that, Rachel. Mentoring played a key role, but I was ready. Louis Pasteur put it best when he said, ' Chance favors the prepared mind.' Remember the rule: keep learning. The more you can contribute, the more likely the right opportunities will show up."

Rachel nodded. "I've been to several really good training classes."

"The right training can help a lot, Rachel, because it can give you the principles and practice, but you learn most from doing the work itself. Take time for projects that give you the opportunity to grow. You just have to keep stretching yourself."

The meeting ended abruptly when Bill's secretary arrived with a message for Rachel. He was waiting and wanted to see her right away.

The next morning Rachel left Jack a note saying she needed to talk about her meeting with Bill. Several hours later, they were huddled in Jack's office. "What's up?" he asked.

"I went to Marketing, and I like the job. I told Bill I wanted to take it. Then, out of the blue, he said he wanted me to think about it. He said I was just hitting my stride here. He started singing my praises, telling me how important I was to the group and suggesting that I would probably not be happy in that job. Now, I don't know what to do. Jack, I'm torn. I didn't sleep at all last night."

"You said you wanted the sales job."

"I do – but it's so tempting to stay here and enjoy all the appreciation I'm getting. I thought I was stuck. Now I'm wondering if I'm walking down the right path by leaving."

Jack nodded sympathetically. "As I said before the choice of path is yours, not mine and not Bill's. I had a similar experience in the sales job I enjoyed so much. In fact, I had been in that job close to five years. There were moments when I was sure I should never leave it. My boss trusted my judgment, and my co-workers constantly sought my advice. It was seductive. One day the boss asked me to take his place putting on a presentation for the whole Marketing Department. I knew the material because I had written most of the talk. Several days later he came to my office and said,' Jack, I've got to tell you, you did such a fine job on that presentation that one of the other managers offered a transfer. Are you interested?'"

"I thought about it for a few minutes and told him I was. He looked crestfallen. He said he hoped I would turn it down. He depended on me, he said. I was flattered but the more I thought about it, the more I thought the offer worth considering. It turned out to be a promotion but even if it hadn't been, I knew I should take it. I was getting stale. I learned two important secrets from that experience. First, don't be seduced by your own importance or by the need to have others singing your praises. Second, don't be impossible to replace. In fact, I'd go a step further. You can help yourself and the organization at the same time by actively coaching your replacement. That way, you can continue to grow and go on to something even more exciting."

Rachel looked relieved. "Thanks, Jack. I knew you could help. I was falling into the same situation you were in. Now I know what to do."

"Be kind to Bill. He'll miss you. So will I."

"Jack, you won't have time to miss me. I look to you for guidance, and as a good friend – and mentor. In fact, have you finished the next chapter of the book? If so, I'm ready to read it."

Grinning, Jack pulled out the manuscript from his desk drawer and handed it to Rachel. "I thought you'd never ask," he said.

Picking up her briefcase, Rachel started toward the door. Then she paused. "Jack, I have something I want you to look at. I'm keeping a journal to capture the main ideas I'm learning from you. Let me show you what I wrote during our discussion today." Intrigued, he looked at the tablet she handed him and read the entry. "I like it!" he said.

JOURNAL ENTRY THREE
To Survive: Know what each part of your work costs and what value it contributes to the organization.

To Succeed: Remember this, if you want to move ahead, don't be impossible to replace.

To Shine: Expand your capabilities by taking on projects that give you the opportunity to learn and grow.

The Fourth Secret

On People You Work With

"No one can whistle a symphony. It takes an orchestra to play it."

~ H.E. Luccock

"Marketing is so different," said Rachel, her voice pensive and uncharacteristically soft. "I think I need some advice before I make a major mistake."

"Let's get together over lunch," said Jack. "I'm really tied up right now, but tomorrow looks good. Will that work for you?"

"I guess it will have to," said Rachel with a sigh. "I started the next chapter in your book, and I see that you're talking about teams and networks, but my concern has to do with supervisors and managers. Do you discuss that in the book?"

"Maybe that's something I need to add," replied Jack. "Tomorrow? How about eleven o'clock?"

■ ■ ■

Lunch was over, and Jack waited patiently as Rachel explained her concerns. "It's not just one person," she said. "The supervisors and managers I've met over in Marketing are nothing like you and Bill. Some are overly controlling as if they assume that I know absolutely nothing about the business – sort of like a new hire," said Rachel, rolling her eyes. "Others are just the reverse," she continued. "They seem to think I should know everything about the business and are not very helpful. I get the impression from some of my coworkers that the place runs rather haphazardly."

"Working with management on any level can be challenging," said Jack, "not only because everybody is different, but frankly some people are better leaders than others. As a matter of fact, if you asked managers what they believe leadership should be, you would get many different answers. For some, the leader's job is inspiring the group with his or her vision of what success looks like and focusing on the strategy to get there. You get the sense that the best leaders appreciate your contributions. They are awesome to work for. For a second group, not quite as strong, being in charge is mostly problem solving. For those in the third and weakest group, it is keeping one's own head above water while avoiding sticky situations."

"That is also true for some supervisors, isn't it?" asked Rachel, leaning forward and clearly interested in the commentary.

"Yes, but on a less complex level depending on the position. The best supervisors focus on taking obstacles out of the way and providing advice and support. They make it clear what they want, and they work with employees individually to help them raise their performance. When you put in that extra effort, they reward you. The middle group focuses on solving problems. Since they tend to concentrate more on the work than the group, their interaction with individual employees is usually limited to giving directions on assignments and performance reviews."

"And the third group?"

"Thank goodness, there are fewer of them. They seem to be universally centered on the wrong things. The big picture is basically a selfie to them. They range from micro-managers who monitor your every move and treat any negative feedback or problem, no matter how trivial, as impacting your career to the so-called bosom buddy types who give you positive feedback and then crucify you on performance if there are any snags in their own or provide *faint praise* for you while taking credit for your work. Then there are the 'screamers.' Their method of solving problems is to increase the volume of their response."

Rachel shook her head. "A screamer! Jack, what do you do with one of those? Run for cover?"

"It's hard to believe adults behave like this, but I had a temporary assignment working for a woman who responded to any perceived stress, no matter how minor, by screaming at the unlucky victim in her office."

"Oh no. How awful."

"I was assigned to head up a team working for her on a rather lengthy and complex report about the future of one aspect of our business. I wrote an opening chapter and an outline laying out our development plan, and I asked her if she would mind looking at the first page and telling me if I was on the right track. Her response was a completely unexpected tirade. Her face turned red and she looked furious. At the top of her lungs, she screamed in a voice that could be heard in the hall, "What is wrong with you? Who do you think I am? I don't have time to hold your hand!""

"What did you do?"

"I stood there until she finished. Then I took a deep breath and said in a very quiet, calm voice, 'I don't think we can work together this way.' That was a response she did not expect. Most people she screamed at told me they generally apologized and got out of her office as quickly as possible. My measured tone and low-key response clearly surprised her. At first she looked stunned, then puzzled. Her reaction was a rather long silence. In the meantime, I just waited. Finally, she apologized explaining that she was under stress. I never had a problem with her after that."

"But what made you do that, Jack? I mean, wasn't it counter-intuitive?"

"Not really. All of us are entitled to respect, no matter who is in charge. I was requiring that from her. The point is, if you get into an emotional situation, take a deep breath. Avoid the temptation to react in kind. Most importantly, don't match the passion of the screamer. Your calmness will generally cause her or him to come back down to earth."

"I'll remember that," said Rachel. "Speaking of respect, I've been hearing from my co-workers about two supervisors, who apparently are close friends. These women have been in their positions for some time and feel threatened when someone new comes in with good reviews. They decide they dislike you on sight, talk behind your back, and make it impossible to get your work in on time if they have to provide input."

"Those are the ones to avoid as much as possible. They need a follower or small group to support their misbehavior. In high school they were called the mean girls. None of the people we've talked about in the third group belong in supervision. That's for sure," said Jack. "One word of caution, Rachel. It's best not to talk with fellow employees about supervisors, leaders, or co-workers. Sometimes people have an axe to grind. Beware of hearing your words repeated or their words attributed to you. In the end, it's best for Rachel, Inc. to focus on her contributions and make her own judgments privately."

"So, Jack, what does one do if he or she finds herself with a supervisor who is in the third group?"

"Are you describing your new supervisor by any chance?"

"Frankly, I'm really not sure if it's Karen or me." She paused for a moment, waiting for Jack to comment. He offered a smile of encouragement, and she went on. "Every time I send her a report or email, she thanks me for the information and attaches a question, note or suggestion for follow-up. It's getting to the point where I hesitate to send her notes. Many of her questions or suggestions are time killers, and they really don't add value. I know details matter, but how much time or effort should I give these questions. Help!"

"Have you discussed it with her?"

"She says everything is important -- that she likes to keep on top of things. One of the other marketers tells me she compares her style to the flight of a helicopter, hovering over the action."

Jack laughed. "Sounds like she may land a bit too often. At any rate, Rachel, it is having an impact on you. I'll tell you how I handled a similar situation, with one caution. First, the method. Begin by dividing the notes into categories. The first is good ideas that you want to follow up on. Do those. The second group is the things that you know are important to Karen. Usually you can tell by phrases like, 'get back to me on this' or expressions like ASAP (as soon as possible). Do those too.

"Then designate a drawer for the ones you see as suggestions," Jack continued. "Date them and see if Karen remembers them. My supervisors rarely did. Their scribbles on my work were passing thoughts. If she comments a second time, you probably need to follow up. If it takes too much of your time, I'd talk with her first. Don't be afraid to suggest an alternative. Most of the time, this strategy works. But be careful. If you're not alert to what's going on, there could be a problem.

"I remember one time when we received an angry letter from a company we no longer used as a supplier. It was from their marketing vice president who threatened to call our president. My boss Roger jotted a note on it that said, 'Put out this fire.' The key word was *fire*, but I wasn't paying attention. I did some research and responded too late. The marketing vice president made the call, and even though he never reached the president, my boss had to talk to him. Roger was steamed and he let me know it."

"What could you have done?"

"I guess I could have told him what I planned to do. He thought I should have called the man, but I didn't think a call from someone at my level would have done anything more than fan the flames."

"I don't think it was fair for Roger to blame you. He was asking you to do the impossible."

"Maybe it wasn't fair, but I learned a long time ago if you worry about making everything fair, you waste time and energy. The important thing is what I learned from it."

"What's that?"

"Sometimes the things that appear the least important to you may be very important to someone else. So, my advice is to read the signals. Begin to listen to Karen so you can tell the difference between what is important and what's interesting, between a request and a passing thought. I failed to give it the proper importance because it wasn't important to me, and it was reflected in my performance review that year."

"But couldn't you have complained about that to the manager?"

"I never considered it. It's an unwritten rule in any company that people who complain get tagged as complainers. That puts everyone in a difficult position. I make one exception to the rule: if you are asked to do something you consider to be wrong. Then you have no choice."

"Has anyone...?"

Jack shook his head. "I think the managers here are decent and honest people. I may not agree with them all the time, but that's the jungle, isn't it."

"What if you have the bad luck to draw one of the supervisors from group three?"

"Each of the ones we talked about in that group presents a different problem. The key to every one of them lies in focusing on your own contributions, becoming part of the team, and building a network. What I have found is there is strength in those three strategies. That's one of the reasons Rachel Inc. needs to operate as a lamp rather than a torch. "

"It's hard not to get rattled though," said Rachel with a sigh.

"It is. If you do get rattled, take a deep breath, back off, and change your focus to the outcome you want. Sometimes, the best you can do is diminish the negative results. Develop a strategy for dealing with this particular person. This is business and you are Rachel Inc. It is a lot easier to do that than try to change someone else. Stand strong without crossing the line. That means when you run into the screaming boss or the one you cannot trust, stay calm and cool. These people usually reveal themselves to others as well and destroy their own reputations.

In parting, Rachel promised to get back with Jack soon to discuss the next chapter. That night Rachel had dinner out with Paul and some friends; however, the following morning was Saturday, and she went back to Jack's book.

■ ■ ■

The Team
I had chosen the path of the Healer, which pleased the Elder because he too was a Healer. He took me to the Wiseman who welcomed me into the group and introduced me to Mali, a sorter, who was to be my teacher. My job was to take baskets loaded with the vegetation collected by the Gatherers and separate the contents by type. My completed basket was to go to a second group of Sorters to be further divided by their uses. Some would be used as balms to be applied directly to wounds or insect bites; some as medications to be taken by mouth; others as rubs for aches and pains.

When I completed my work, I watched a group of Healers preparing medications. Some were puncturing the bark from a brownish gray tree to extract copal. Others were grinding leaves of the konoya plant to make tea for treating colds and sore throat. This work looked more interesting to me than sorting, so I went to Mali. "I don't like sorting anymore," I said. "It's too menial. I want to work with the Medicine Makers."

Mali smiled. "You have much to discover where you are, Keli. There are many more roots, berries, flowers, and shrubs than the ones you have worked with so far. Be patient; pay attention to details; learn from those around you, and when you have proven yourself as a Sorter, you will be given more difficult work to do."

Several days later, I noticed that Manu, a Sorter who was usually friendly, did not respond when I greeted him. Later that day I saw him talking to Tari, another Sorter, and pointing in my direction. That evening I asked Tari if she knew what was wrong. She responded, "Manu saw you helping Koita split the cashew nuts. He thinks you should have asked if one of the Sorters needed your help before you went to help the Medicine Makers." Puzzled, I repeated the story to Mali. "You are bright and quick to learn," Mali told me. "You have asked for my counsel, so think of this; those who work beside you may also need your help. Do not forget to join hands with them lest they see you as an outsider."

■ ■ ■

The following afternoon Jack stopped by Rachel's office. "Well?" he asked, expectantly.

"I haven't finished Chapter 4 yet, but I'm interested in why you think teamwork is so important."

"Because, you cannot be a star until you've recognized the importance of being a team member. Rachel, have you ever watched a winning basketball team? A great player who is not a team member can score many points, but it's no guarantee that the team will prevail. A great player who is a team member, however raises the level of play for everyone. I believe it's the same way in business. The secret is to stay aware of the impact of our actions on those around us.

He continued, "Manu was angry with Keli for two reasons: first, because he didn't treat the team as important when he went to help the other group before the team had completed all the baskets; second, because he violated a norm. Violating a rule can get you in trouble with your boss, but violating a norm hurts you with your team."

"I know what a norm is," said Rachel. "It's an unspoken rule in a work group. It's eating lunch together on a Friday, or taking turns doing some of the less pleasant work. I think Manu was out of line by the way he handled the situation. I would have told Keli about it rather than whispering to others."

"You're right," said Jack shaking his head in agreement. "He probably violated a norm as well. And he clearly didn't understand what we discussed the other day."

"You mean about being tagged as a complainer?"

"Exactly. Complaining about another person, unless it is about something serious, makes you look powerless. What works in Manu's favor is that he clearly has been there longer than Keli, so the team recognizes his value. Now, it's Keli's responsibility to earn his place on the team."

Just then Jack's cell rang. Glancing down, he said, "Have to take this. Call you later." As Jack closed the door behind him, Rachel decided to read more of Chapter 4 that evening.

■ ■ ■

The Team (continued)
I was bothered about the situation with Manu for several reasons: First, I could see our differences affecting the group. Second, it is hard to solve a problem with someone who refuses to speak. I felt Manu was being stubborn and unreasonable. When I asked Tari what to do, she suggested I talk to Pola, a Senior Healer who was known for giving excellent advice on all sorts of matters regarding work, health, and relationships. Pola agreed to help.

That afternoon Pola, Manu, and I met at the pond. Pola asked each of us to describe what happened while the other listened without speaking. We were allowed to ask each other questions, but we couldn't interrupt or contradict each other. That was hard. Then Pola asked each of us to say one thing we valued about the other. I told Manu I liked the way he was willing to share secrets that made the work go faster. He said he appreciated the way I listened and asked questions. After that each of us described one thing the other could do to improve our relationship. That was easy. Manu wanted me to help the team first. I nodded eagerly. I wanted Manu to tell me directly if I bungled again. He looked down for a moment and then extended his hands in a gesture of apology. I did the same. Pola smiled. "I think this is a good first step," she said.

After that, we met a number of times at the end of our evening meal and walked by the river. With each successive meeting, we became more open in discussing how things were going between us. After a while, when our discussions began to cover a much broader range of topics, Pola and Mali asked if they could walk along with us. Then I felt like a true member of the team. In fact, we became so close that I was heartsick to learn that Manu was moving to a Healer Gatherers' group in a small village miles away. We agreed to send messages by runners moving between those areas. The morning Manu was leaving he drew a map in the dirt to show us how to get to the village. We embraced and agreed to visit each other often.

■ ■ ■

"I like the way that turned out," said Rachel. She was seated opposite Jack in a small meeting room having a late afternoon snack of cookies and hot tea. "Now that Manu and Keli are separated, I wonder if they will keep in touch."

"Sure they will," said Jack, taking another chocolate chip cookie from the basket Rachel had brought him. "And even though Keli is sad, he will probably soon realize the value Manu has as a member of his network."

"You've always had a great network, Jack. How do you use it?"

"Information, contacts, getting resources. If I have a project and want to know what others think about a product or who might give me the information I need, it helps to be able to ask someone. Often there's a chain. My source might not know, but she might be aware of someone who does. The answer is frequently a few phone calls away, but you have to know who to call."

"If I'm getting ready to go into a meeting and there are some people I don't know who will participate in making a decision important to me, I get in touch with one of my network to get some insight into how that person might respond. Perhaps I want to meet someone from another department, " continued Jack. "It helps to know someone who can pave the way. One thing is for sure, my friends have come to my rescue more than once."

"Do you have a network outside the company too?"

"Yes. That's also important. "

"How do you create an outside network?"

"Well, it is easier today than it used to be with social networking. There are a number of websites, you probably know them better than I do, where you can link with people who have similar interests. My caution is -- don't depend on them for a solid network. Use them to continue building relationships. Making friends with a few keystrokes and revealing information about yourself may seem enticing, but they are no substitute for creating the kind of relationships that can support you when you need information or connections."

Rachel smiled. "I do have friends that I have met on social networks, but I also have a few hundred people added to my network that I really don't know. "

"Nothing beats face to face communication," said Jack. "Social networks are great tools to keep in touch with family that is far away or friends that you have known a long time. It also can be an aid to sustaining your network. Just don't rely on them for the contacts you need to develop. Take opportunities to meet people on shared projects, task forces, business meetings and training sessions. Remember, the person you meet casually might be someone who can be important down the road. Most important, don't rely exclusively on texting, email, and telephones. You'd be surprised how much easier it is to work through challenges and differences when you've met someone face to face. I've used all these opportunities to build a network, and I've never regretted the time it took to do it. Computers are great tools, but they should come with warning signs: don't rely on them exclusively to develop a relationship."

"I know you're right," said Rachel. "My biggest problem with face to face encounters is remembering names. You're so good at that, Jack. How in the world----?"

"I made it a point to learn the tricks experts have devised for remembering names. You can find books, audio tapes, or look on YouTube, and other online means to develop memory skills. Even so, I try to make a few notes after I meet people for the first time. Often I ask people to repeat their names. Most people are struggling with the same problem, so they are relieved to ask me to repeat mine."

"So the more activities I'm a part of, the more I build my network. Right?"

"Absolutely. And that's one of the reasons I told you, a while back, that hard work is important, but it isn't enough. It's networks and mentors and building relationships across all sorts of boundaries that finally make the difference. They are the sources of light."

JOURNAL ENTRY FOUR
To Survive: Pay attention to the leadership and supervisory styles of those you work with.

To Succeed: Become an active contributor to the team.

To Shine: Build networks on and off the job.

The Fifth Secret

On Choices, Pitfalls, and Traps

"In adversity, remember to keep an open mind."

HORACE

Two taps on the door to Rachel's office. "Come on in," she said, almost grimly.

The door opened. "Good morning. Hope I'm not interrupting," said Jack with a smile. "You've been hard to reach the last couple of weeks. I admit it, I'm checking up on you. Am I in the doghouse?" He paused and looked at her. "Where's that happy Rachel look?"

"You know it's not you," said Rachel, finally softening her expression. "Frankly, I should have stopped by to see you long ago. I've been on a project. Now it's 'down the tubes' and I hate to dump on you."

"I'm here now. Dump away."

Rachel leaned forward. "I must admit I'm feeling disgruntled--and it is a long story. It all started a couple of weeks ago when Rich Cargell, Karen's manager, told me PWE was starting this year's Spirit of Volunteerism campaign. He told me all the usual stuff--good for community relations, great for morale--you know what I mean."

Jack nodded. "It really is a worthwhile cause."

"I know," said Rachel. "Rich said all the PWE businesses were represented on the committee and asked me to represent Marketing.

He said the two previous campaigns hadn't been very exciting, and management was looking for some sparkle. I can tell you honestly, Jack, I was flattered."

"And you're just the person to add that sparkle. So what happened?"

"Shortly after I met with Rich, I received a notice of the first committee meeting from Marjorie Anderson of Human Resources, the committee chairperson. I was really fired up by what Rich said. Marjorie was very encouraging. 'No limits,' she said. By the second meeting, the committee had a list of recommendations -- things like volunteering to teach a critical thinking class at a local high school or of offering a semester of science at a middle school. We thought about sponsoring a debate or some other activity to increase understanding of local government. There were other good ideas offered. The committee divided into groups to sell the top three ideas. Cindy and I chose sponsoring a music and art festival."

"Sounds like a very aggressive committee. What kind of support did you get?"

" Marjorie was enthusiastic. She asked us to flesh the idea out. To promote our idea, we went to a local chamber music group, and they agreed to put on a musical interlude in the cafeteria. We agreed on Friday about one month later. The date is coming up next week. Cindy and I felt that would give us plenty of time to get approval and work the logistics. Then we visited three art galleries and got the owners to commit to thematic art shows in the lobby on three successive weeks. They even committed to provide local artists to come and talk about their work. To top it off, we found two excellent speakers--Estella Rivera, an expert on the music and art of our city, and Jackson Steel, a well-known designer who could discuss our architectural history. We knew these activities would promote interest in the campaign and get volunteers for the festival."

"Awesome!" said Jack. "You went to a lot of work to put this together. How did Marjorie and the rest of the committee react?"

"Marjorie was ecstatic. Other members of the committee were impressed, but they were busy on the other two recommendations. We were all going like a house afire."

"I get the impression," said Jack softly, "that someone doused the flames."

Rachel nodded. "Last Friday I called Marjorie to find out who would be in charge of setting up the stage in the cafeteria for the chamber music this Friday. She hedged and stumbled around a bit, then asked if I could come to her office. So I did. When I got there she told me she had finally met with the management group on Wednesday, and they had said the art could go on exhibit, but we could not have the chamber music in the cafeteria. They weren't sure we needed the speakers either. I was stunned. I mean these people were donating their time in the interest of the community. This was just one week before the start-up date. When I asked her why, Marjorie said she thought management must have had a smaller plan in mind from the beginning. Jack, she never told us that. No limits? Then she said she had meant there was no limit on ideas. That's a cop out! She knew what we were doing. Cindy and I kept her informed from the start with emails and text messages. All that work. All those commitments -- and waiting until Wednesday. She had only two jobs to do: head the committee and work with management. If she had done her job, this wouldn't have happened."

Jack thought a moment before responding. He shook his head sympathetically. "So management objected to the music in the cafeteria. Did they have a problem with putting it somewhere else?"

"Marjorie said they would have to give it some consideration. What does that mean! Anyway, we were placed in a difficult situation. I was the one who begged the people to come and now I may have to beg off. The other committee members ran into similar brick walls. We're all angry and disgusted. I must have gotten five calls since last Friday from other members. My heart is pounding, Jack. I don't know what to do."

"Sounds like you have three problems: first, to find out what can be salvaged from the work you've already done; second, to mollify the people from the community who have made these commitments if their roles cannot be salvaged; and third, to understand what management really had in mind so you can help the committee sort this out. Have I missed any?"

"Yes, Jack. There's one more. We are having a meeting tomorrow, and I'm wondering if I should nail Marjorie. She deserves it. What do you think?"

"If you're asking my advice, I'd say don't fall into the trap of talking to her when you're angry. And don't nail Marjorie in a meeting in front of everyone. What would that gain?"

"I might feel better for one thing. Jack, she gave us bad signals and disrupted the work of everyone--and I think she should know that."

"So do I, but feedback like that is best delivered in private. Before you come down too hard, you probably want to give Marjorie a chance to explain what happened. Then, provide her with information about the impact that her failing to get good information has had on you, the people in the community, and the other committee members. Clearly, as the chair of the committee she had a responsibility -- and even if management gave her a last minute surprise, she could have done a much better job of handling it. At the same time, don't forget, you might have to work with her again, and chastising her in front of everyone won't help."

"I know you're right, but it'll be hard to back off. She already knows I'm not happy about the whole thing. What do I say to her that doesn't sound like I'm taking her on?"

"Use soft words, Rachel. Tell her you're *puzzled* by what happened and you'd *like to understand*. Tell her you're *disappointed*, and you've been *wondering* if it might have helped if she had involved management earlier. Words like that help set the stage for a discussion, not a scolding (even though you're sorely tempted to do it). What you are trying to do is get into a problem solving mode. Look,

I'm not suggesting you let Marjorie off the hook -- just that you don't come across in a way that you'll regret later."

"It always helps to talk to you. I'll bet you have a chapter on situations like this."

"I do. Remember early in the book when the Elder warned Keli about the hidden dangers of the jungle? I've mentioned some of those in my next chapter. If you like, I'll drop it by on my way to lunch. I'd like to get your thoughts on it."

Several hours later, Jack dropped by on his way to a meeting, leaving the manuscript on Rachel's desk. Anticipating its arrival, she had rushed down to the cafeteria, picked up a sandwich and soda and returned to her office. Now with lunch in front of her, Rachel settled back in her chair, kicked off her shoes and began reading.

Avoiding the Pitfalls
We had been walking for about two hours, searching for shemane fern. The Elder was ahead, and I walked behind for the path was narrow and overgrown. It was an oppressively hot morning, and the air was very still. We were searching for a place to rest when I came to a small area where the growth was not as dense. I called to him and started to sit down, but he turned quickly and grabbed my arm. "Don't move!" he said.

I was startled. "Don't you wish to stop for a moment?" I asked.

"Not by this liana," he said, shaking his head. "It can give you a painful burn. That's why it is called a fire plant. You must be very careful, Keli. There are many dangers in the jungle for one who is unaware."

We continued walking for the next few minutes. Finally, we reached the river and sat on a fallen log several feet from the edge. "Have you heard what Pola has asked me to do?"

"I have. You are to go to the city with Pardo, the Trader, and Lutar, the Toolmaker, to buy clothing, blankets, and other supplies for the villagers. It is an honor to be chosen."

"Pola feels I know a lot about the city because I was raised there."

"That is only one of the reasons you were chosen. You have shown a great willingness to help."

"I understand. Pola told me, but...."

"But?"

"But I have a problem, and I am not sure what to do. Pardo came to me the other night and told me he had spoken with several of the other traders. They think we should ask the villagers what other things they would like us to bring back."

"And?"

"Pardo has asked me to keep this from Lutar. He says because the Toolmaker is old and close to the Chief, he will not agree to this. I am in the middle, and I don't know what to do."

"Whose mission is this?"

"Father, I have been told it is the Chief's mission."

"Who chose you for this mission?"

"Pola says it was the Shaman."

"What is the reason for the mission?"

I was exasperated, but because I loved the Elder, I chose not to show it. "To buy the supplies needed for the tribe."

The Elder looked at me and smiled. "You are probably wondering why I am asking you these questions. Let me put this another way. Suppose you go to the villagers. Each of them tells you what he or she wants. For Mali, it is a colorful skirt; for Bari, some ribbons to adorn his arrows; for little Tani, a special treat. You make your list. Then you say, 'Give me something so I may pay for this in the city,' and each tells you, 'Go to the Chief and get something to trade.'"

"And what would the Chief say?"

"He would say, 'Why did you ask the villagers? For now, they are happy. Soon they will be disappointed.' So what would you say to that, Keli?"

"I don't know, Father," I sighed.

"My Son, there are many pitfalls in the jungle. You might trip over this log and fall into the river and drown or go fishing and step on the flat fish that stings You understand these dangers. There are other perils that lie in wait for the unwary. You must learn to spot these too."

"What are they?"

"For one thing, be wary when one team member tries to pit you against another. Always understand what the purpose of the mission is. Following the way of Pardo instead of Lutar would be a mistake. Lutar knows the reason the Tribal Chief is sending you to the city. It is not to gratify the wishes of each of us as individuals but to supply the needs of the tribe as a whole. Pardo does not seem to understand this. So which should you follow?"

"Lutar."

"Very good. Now because you are a bright young man, you have avoided the second pitfall-- acting in haste."

"But what if Pardo calls me 'coward'"?

"What if he does? Those words mean nothing. Act on what you know is true."

"Should I go to Lutar and tell him what happened?"

"No. Keep your own counsel. There will be other times when you and Pardo will see the same."

"Should I go to Pardo and tell him he should not have done this"?

"If you wish, my Son. But if you do, avoid the harshness that comes from pronouncing yourself right and another wrong. This too is a pitfall, for even though it may be true, it creates needless enemies. Always remember, next time you might be wrong."

"I will remember. One more question, Father. Could one be overly cautious?"

"Yes," said the Elder, "that is another pitfall, for in our failure to act, decisions are made without us. Thus, we give up our freedom to choose. We must be thoughtful but not afraid."

For a few minutes we sat in silence. Then my gaze was drawn to the river where two white herons emerged from behind the overhanging tree in search of fish. I walked to the water's edge. This was a part of the river I had never seen before. The water looked cool and inviting, but who could know if black caiman or flesh-eating fish lay beneath the surface.

As if to read my thoughts, the Elder spoke. "You have seen the tall birds fishing without fear. That is a good sign. Enjoy the river, Keli. Just be aware that it holds dangers as well as delights."

For a moment I stood there. Then I walked boldly in.

■ ■ ■

Jack picked up the telephone on the first ring. The caller ID said the voice on the other end of the line would be Rachel's. "Hi," he said. "I wasn't expecting to hear from you so soon." The minute she responded he could tell things were better. "You sound like the old Rachel."

"Watch it. I'm not sure how I like your use of *old* in front of my name. I finished the chapter during lunch, and I've had quite an afternoon. Do you have time to talk?"

Jack glanced at his watch. He had a meeting in ten minutes that promised to take the rest of the day. Tomorrow morning would be out as well because of Rachel's Volunteerism Committee meeting. They arranged to meet for coffee in Jack's office the following afternoon. "Actually, that'll work out fine," said Rachel. "We can talk about the book, and I'll also be able to tell you about my talk with Marjorie. By then the committee meeting will be history, so you'll get a full report on that too. I now have a plan--so keep your fingers crossed."

"Can I have a headline on the Marjorie talk? I hate to wait that long."

"Okay, Jack, here's your headline. 'Talks progressing between Rachel and Marjorie. Each side claiming victory.' Bye now."

He smiled and put down the phone. Rich was right. Rachel did sparkle.

It was just after two the next day. Jack was standing by the window, looking out when Rachel walked in. "All right, mystery lady. Tell me what happened. The suspense is killing me."

"Yesterday when I read the chapter, there were certain things that hit me, particularly the questions the Elder asked Keli about the purpose of the mission. All of a sudden I realized what happened in the committee. In some ways we got sidetracked by the desire to have everything complete and forgot to check with management, who gave us the mission, to make sure we were heading in the right direction."

"That's an important lesson, Rachel. It is a good idea to try out your ideas before you get overinvested in them. And being clear about the purpose, scope, and boundaries of an assignment is vital to your success. Ah, but I digress. Sorry. So tell me, what did you do?"

"Let me go through my thoughts first. Something you told me, perhaps in passing, came back to me. Instead of throwing everything out, why not see what could be salvaged. So I got with Cindy and together we planned a strategy for our meeting with Marjorie. You had encouraged me to give her feedback in private, but Cindy and I were partners in the venture, so we decided to go in together."

"Good decision."

"I was also influenced by two other points in the story. The Elder tells Keli not to sound harsh – and Cindy and I agreed with that. We were both nervous in a way going in to give Marjorie feedback was like when Keli walked into the river, feeling there might not be any crocodiles – but you never know."

"So what happened?"

"Our strategy was a good one. First, we would offer Marjorie some helpful feedback. She needed to know how at least two members of the committee felt about what had happened in time to do something about it. When the project was over, it would be too late to make amends."

"How did that go?"

"Probably a little better than we thought it would. She wasn't eager to hear our thoughts, but once we got the discussion going, she admitted feeling that she had not done the proposal justice. We agreed with her – but nicely, Jack."

"Good for you. I think too many people try to take the sting out of feedback and spoil a good opportunity for growth on both sides; that's a way of treating people as if they are too weak to hear the truth and too powerless to change. I'm glad you didn't fall into that trap."

"Me too, but I must admit at one point it was tempting. I felt sorry for Marjorie, but she stood up pretty well considering she was *outwomanned*. Once we finish the feedback, we did get into some problem solving. Both Cindy and I agreed we might have gone overboard a bit, but our product was excellent for PWE and its Spirit of Volunteerism campaign. In fact, we felt it important that in the name of good community relations the company welcome both of the speakers who are thought leaders in the community. Both had agreed to participate in the Music and Arts Festival if management chose to sponsor it. Marjorie said she would take another stab at it, reminding management that backing off now could have a negative effect."

"Good thinking, Rachel. You and Cindy are a dynamite team."

She grinned. "As for the chamber music, we asked Marjorie why the objection to having it in the cafeteria. She said she would find out and call us back. Later I got a phone call from her. Cindy was rushing into my office, so I assumed correctly that Marjorie had called her first. Anyway, the latest is – the speakers are back on, and they will even be introduced by a member of management. How's that for a turnaround? Management had not intended to have us cancel the chamber music – only to move it from the cafeteria. They felt it would be intrusive for the people eating lunch and impolite to the people playing. So I won't have to call them after all and tell them they been canceled. They will play in the auditorium instead. Cindy and I will have to do some real advertising to make sure people know. You've got to come, Jack. It's Friday from 11 – 12."

"I'll be there. So tell me, what will you write in your journal?"
"Here it is, Jack."

JOURNAL FIVE
To survive: Understand the purpose, scope and boundaries of every task.

To succeed: Be honest without being harsh and courageous without being foolhardy.

To shine: If you want to solve a problem, avoid criticizing another in public or blaming another --anywhere. Remember the old saying, "There's always plenty of blame to go around."

The Sixth Secret

On Perspective

"Our point of view depends on where we are standing."

"Getting back to the jungle, do you plan to write about turf situations?" asked Rachel.

"Why? What's happening?" asked Jack.

"Problems between headquarters and the field. The information flow is so poor that Karen asked to visit several of our field locations and see what can be done. The problem right now is scheduling my visit. They have been dragging their feet about timing. I think they're reluctant to have me come. Karen says that's typical."

"Looks like an opportunity to me."

"I'd like to think it is. Sometimes it feels as if we are more in competition with each other than with other companies."

"Sometimes we are. That's a great subject for...."

"Let me guess," said Rachel, extending her hand, palm upward. "It's a new chapter."

He grinned. "You know me. And you're a great editor too. It's that reciprocity thing we talked about earlier."

■ ■ ■

The next three days were hectic for Rachel. Paul and Brad were off on a fishing trip. That helped. After several meetings with Karen and numerous phone calls, her trip had been expanded to three field locations. Rachel had been too busy to read the book, but now, wedged between two rather large people on a small airplane, she began Chapter Six.

Resolving Conflicts
One morning just after sunrise, the Shaman called all the Healers together. We gathered beside the hill to hear his words. Tomorrow, he told us, the Tribal Council would go to the mountain top to make plans for the months ahead. As Chief Healer, it was his responsibility to prepare the Healer Wiseman for this meeting. The Shaman asked us to meet within our four groups (Sorters, Gatherers, Medicine Makers, and Counselors) today to discuss anything we felt important for the Council to consider. At sunset, representatives from each of the four groups would convey our ideas to the Shaman and the Elders. Those they deemed critical to the plan would be shared with the Healer Wiseman who sat on the Tribal Council. Like the Shaman, the Chief Hunter, Trader and Toolmaker were conducting similar meetings.

At the end of the meeting, the Shaman gave us a chance to ask questions. I wanted to learn more about the Tribal Council and how it works but decided to wait until the meeting ended and ask Mali, for she was the Senior Sorter and understood many things about the tribe that I did not.

She explained, "There are five people who sit on the Council: the Tribal Chief and the Wisemen from the four paths."

"But why do the Healers have a Wiseman and a Shaman too?"

"Because the Wiseman has climbed the tall mountain, he sees things others may not. Each of the Wisemen have made this climb and each is a valued counselor to the Tribal Chief. The Shaman has climbed to the top of a great hill and helps us in our daily work to become better at what we do."

"But do the Shaman or the Chief Hunter, Chief Trader or the Chief Toolmaker go to the meeting on the mountain top?"

"No. They are needed here to make important decisions. Should the Council seek advice from one or all of them, they have only to send a runner from the mountain."

"And what of the Elders? Do they ever go?"

"Only when there are significant issues related to their experience. Remember, the most important work is here, not up on the mountain top. The Tribal Chief has said many times that it is the efforts of villagers like you and me that make the tribe prosperous."

"What do they talk about in the meeting?" Tari asked.

They make decisions that affect our survival: supplies, food, clothing, housing, medicine. They are concerned with all the needs of the village. They make plans in case something happens like a fire or a storm. They resolve conflicts among us. This is a very important council.

With that, we turned our attention to the task of preparing for the meeting with the Shaman. Dor, one of the Sorters, spoke. "I have noticed lately that the pokeweed berries look withered and dry. Yesterday I mentioned this to one of the Gatherers. He said the Hunters knocked them over or cut them down with their knives when they were tracking the cougars."

A younger Sorter nodded. "I have wondered about this too. What is causing it to happen now? We have not had this problem before."

Mali responded, " I think the Hunters are using new trails to track the cougars. I remember something like this happened several years ago. After the Shaman discussed it with the Chief Hunter, things improved for a while. We should ask the Shaman if this new problem should go to the Tribal Council. The poke wood berries are the best medicine for head parasites, but they cannot be used if they are withered or dried up." Everyone agreed to ask the Shaman if the Hunters could find a different trail to track the cougars.

Another question arose concerning the Healers in our small village to the north. I perked up because that was where Manu had been sent. It seemed they had located a wonderful source for the rosy periwinkles that cured sore throat, wasp stings, and reduced fever but were unwilling to share this information with anyone from our village. Mali felt the Shaman would want to know this, but it would probably be resolved by the Healers and not the Tribal Council.

That evening, Mali and I met with the Shaman. He listened intently to our concerns. "I will convey this to our Wiseman. Perhaps he can work *something out at the Tribal Council," he said. "Know this, if the Council is forced to choose between our needs and those of the Hunters, we cannot expect them to sacrifice food and skins for medicine. Head parasites can be a problem, but they do not threaten one's life. However, we will ask what concessions can be made to help us."* Concerning the rosy periwinkles, he suggested the Healers send me to visit Manu. *"Friends can work things out."*

Mali was insistent. "They are a small village. They must do as we tell them, mustn't they?"

The Shaman smiled. "Yes, they must. Perhaps next time, they will not search so hard, or, if they find the periwinkles in a new place, they will keep silent because they remember how they were treated. That is why good intentions often lead to bad results. It's far better to get their willing help. A better question would be 'how did they find the flowers' not 'where.' Send Keli."

Rachel was so wrapped up in the story that she was surprised when the pilot told the stewardess to prepare for landing. She looked at her watch. It was just after three. Hopefully she could catch Jack at the office. She had some questions that might impact her meeting in the morning. He was clearly surprised to hear her voice.

"I thought you were on your way to Atlanta."

"I'm there. In an hour I catch my next flight. Now I have a question about what you said about 'turf battles.'"

"Shoot."

"The Shaman tells Keli and Mali if the Council is forced to choose between the Hunters and the Healers, the Healers would lose. Does that carry over into PWE?"

"I believe it does. To understand the 'pecking order' in any organization, look at who gets the most influential positions. You see in a turf battle, the outcome is rarely in doubt. Human Resources, Finance, and other support organizations can never hope to beat out the departments that bring in the money (the Hunters). The exception is where there are legal or regulatory issues. Therefore, it really is better not to engage on an unequal battlefield."

"Are you saying support departments should always give in?"

"No. If the support organization can come up with a compelling argument that shows its interest takes precedence because of company-wide implications, it can win. You've got to realize though, when you hit the battlefield you use up your 'silver bullets' which are generally in short supply."

"So, settle on the front?"

"Someone very wise once told me, 'If you are going to lose, yield the point graciously. Collaborate whenever you can. If you can't do that, pick your battles.' It's foolish to fight over anything unless it is a matter of principle or profit. And don't forget, it's even more important to be gracious in winning. *People might forget the outcome, but they never forget how you treated them.* Either way, you build up credits--positive or negative."

"You made an interesting point about field offices when you said we can't tell them what to do. On this trip, I feel like Keli being asked to talk to Manu and straighten things out with the smaller village."

"Field offices and headquarters rarely see eye to eye," said Jack. "To the field, headquarters is like an empire wanting to control its subjects from a distance. To headquarters, the field is like a colony, at once asserting independence and at the same time asking for support. The point I was making is that you cannot control anyone or anything from a distance. If you don't believe me, try calling Brad when you're on a business trip and telling him to spend the night studying, stay away from television, and go to bed early. What a joke!"

"Thanks, Jack. I've got a plane to catch and a lot to think about tonight. I might need to consider a bit of strategy revision before tomorrow. Oh, and by the way, I really enjoyed Chapter 6. Are you going to take your readers to the mountain top to hear the Tribal Council in action?"

"That will forever remain a mystery. See you when you get back. I'll be eager to hear how things went."

"And you will. Be back next week. Wish me luck."

Once again in the air, Rachel took out her journal and wrote:

JOURNAL ENTRY SIX

To survive: Choose your battles carefully.

To succeed: Understand how conflicts are resolved in your organization.

To shine: Always remember, in any conflict, people may forget who won or lost, but they never forget how you treated them.

The Seventh Secret

On Perception and Meaning

"We don't see things as they are. We see things as we are."

Anais Nin

*K*eli sat on a fallen tree limb looking out at the water. His shoulders drooped forward, and the Elder could see that he was lost in thought. "I have been looking for you, Keli," he said. "Ah, I can see you are troubled," he added.

"They do not understand me," responded Keli. "I overheard Leya telling Pola that I do not fit in, that my ways are too much like the people that live in the city."

"Did you hear what Pola told her?"

"No. I didn't want to hear anymore, so I walked away."

"I understand, Keli, but Pola told me that Leya's remarks came when she learned that you were selected to join the Gatherers. Leya has been a Sorter longer than you, and she is disappointed that you were chosen over her. That decision was made by the Head Gatherer because you are inquisitive and learn quickly. Pola told Leya that your experiences are different from hers and from the others who were not raised in the city, but that is no reason to condemn you. Each of us has experiences that make us different from one another."

. . .

Rachel shook her head in agreement as she read these words. Her trip to the field had been an eye opener. She had been stunned by the behavior of some of the young professionals. She had been told that they were technologically very bright, but in the meeting where she had made her presentation, some of the younger employees did not seem to be interested in information about the company, its future, or the role headquarters played.

After the meeting, the Employee Relations Manager had shown her around the facility. Few appeared to be working. There were some employees focused on their mobile phones and several young people were slumped over their desks. They looked sloppy to Rachel dressed in their blue jeans and tee shirts and wearing tennis shoes without socks. What a way to dress for work, she had thought. PWE used to have some requirements for leisure wear at the office. As they walked through the broad open spaces of the floor, she had overheard one of them complaining about sitting through boring meetings led by " headquarters types" interfering with their schedules. "Those people need to stay in their fancy offices and email us if they have something they think we need to know," was one comment she remembered hearing from a disheveled looking stringy-haired blonde with her back to the aisle talking to someone on her cell phone.

"I think I might have been the boring person she was referring to," said Rachel.

"Don't take it personally," responded Jack, "the good news is that not all the young people today are alike. Some are much more what we would think of as traditional. However, there is a large group of young people, Millennials or Generation Y or the Net Generation, as some call them, who do not share our points of view. Because of shaky economic conditions, the sense of reduced opportunity that dominates the news on the internet, and the loss of faith in institutions we grew up with, their lives are different from ours--just as Keli's life experiences are different from Leya's. Many are still living at home, not getting married as young, and focused on living for today rather than seeing a career as thirty or forty years with the same company."

"Might I add, they seem to have an inflated view of themselves."

Jack laughed. "I know what you mean. They are more outspoken, less patient. Many of them are not prepared to start at the bottom and work their way up like I did. They are no respecters of gray hair. Their mentors are their peers. Another big change is the importance they attach to the work environment. They will not work in surroundings that do not suit them."

"So recruiting them must be a challenge," said Rachel.

"Perhaps an even bigger challenge is keeping them," added Jack. "If the career ladder doesn't appeal, the daily life at work had better offer rewards. That's why so many big companies are turning their offices into campuses complete with amenities like parks, exercise facilities, swimming pools and coffee shops. Your generation (Generation X) and mine (The Baby Boomers), had a lot more patience."

"Why do organizations put up with them?"

"Many are smart, talented, and can work with technology because they grew up speaking the language. In today's world, those are important assets. They are very diverse and net oriented. Just look at how social media has exploded. That is the focus of so much of their attention."

"Fran Johnson, the manager of one group, says she has a hard time making her staff employees report to work. Some of the young people call in at the drop of a hat saying they don't feel well and do not plan to come today -- or, they leave early with the excuse that they have something important to do. She told me if she tries to insist by saying she is short-handed, their response is, 'I quit.' Some leave for lunch and don't come back to work."

"What you describe is, unfortunately, a universal problem," said Jack.

Rachel sighed. "I'm hoping at some point they will grow up into responsible adults. If not, I fear for my golden years."

Jack smiled in agreement. "I think too many organizations are leaning toward an 'anything goes' attitude in order to appeal to the younger Millennials. They lose sight of the need for a disciplined work force to actually get things done. It is important to be responsive and to understand how events shape our attitudes about everything--including work. At the same time, there's something I learned a long time ago from one of my favorite books, *You Really Oughta Wanna*: people do what gets rewarded. What leaders need to ask themselves is are they overcompensating for this different generation by rewarding lack of self-discipline when they should be rewarding the best in people."

Rachel nodded in agreement. "That happened to me in a previous job. The person who was in charge of placing television sets in key locations once a week to make sure the Company President's weekly briefing was heard by all employees didn't do it half the time. Instead of consequences for her, they turned around and gave the job to me because I always did the work assigned, no matter how unrewarding."

"So, she was rewarded for being lackluster, and you were punished for performing. What a strategy!"

"I was relieved when they finally decided to drop the whole thing," said Rachel. "Speaking of rewards and consequences, one thing that seems to be prevalent in this new world is that words have become weapons and they no longer mean anything. These young people are growing up at a time when terms like *sexist* and *bigot* have lost their true meaning because they are thrown around too easily as a way to condemn people for having a different opinion. "

"Listening is hard work, especially when the other person is equally committed to his point of view. Demeaning others is a way of dismissing those with whom we disagree. Some people are so invested in their own ideas they refuse to modify their opinions or even worse, entertain the thought that they may be wrong. In some respects, their expectations create their reality. Thus, you become a 'headquarters type' and your input is easily dismissed."

"So," said Rachel, "by changing the meaning of words, we can then say the other person is automatically wrong?"

"That's the whole idea. We replace rational thought with opinions and feelings. We replace responding, a thoughtful process, with reacting, an emotional instinct."

"But doesn't that mean anything goes?" asked Rachel. "If you can change the meaning of words and react to them emotionally, then what happens to our shared value system, our culture?"

Jack shook his head. "No, certain values and beliefs inform our society and we should stand up for them without fear. Words like *liberty*, *inalienable rights* and *freedom of speech*, rather than push-button terms like *homophobe* or *xenophobe*, form the basis of our shared values and beliefs. We do not have to accept their being brushed aside out of fear of offending someone. Truly, some benefit from using such language, but that's what I find offensive."

"Oh good grief," sighed Rachel, "I have been to the doctor's office many times and I have never seen anyone in the waiting room who needed to see the doctor because he or she was offended. Everyone finds something offensive. I say 'Merry Christmas.' Some get offended even by that. I say, 'Get over it.' If you respond, 'Happy Holidays,' I'll get over that too, and we can still be friends."

"You make a good point, " said Jack. "We should not try to force our individual values on others. There's a difference. That's because there's a confusion between shared values and beliefs, like those that represent our country, for example, referring to it as 'the land of the free and the home of the brave' and individual values like those particular to our group."

"But how does diversity come in?"

"Actually, it's such an important part of our culture that I am writing an individual chapter on community. Our shared values and beliefs as a nation do not interfere with our strong commitments to diversity. As a nation of immigrants, one of those shared values is respecting differences. When we refuse to stand up for free speech, we are actually denying the value of diversity."

"Well, how will Keli deal with the attitude of Leya?"

"With the help of the Elder, he will grow in understanding and be a role model for her and others in the tribe."

JOURNAL ENTRY SEVEN
To survive: Choose to respond rationally rather than reacting emotionally to those who disagree with you. Avoid using "push-button" language.

To succeed: Understand the difference between shared and individual values.

To shine: Recognize that each of us has life experiences that make us different from one another.

The Eighth Secret

On Character and Reputation

"Character is like a tree and reputation like a shadow. The shadow is what we think of it; the tree is the real thing."

– Abraham Lincoln

It was several weeks before Rachel and Jack got back together, busy weeks with Jack off on a business trip and Rachel hard at work on several projects. Returning Chapter 7 gave Rachel a chance to tell Jack about her latest performance appraisal. She beamed as she recounted how Karen told her of several highly complementary calls she had received from managers of the field locations Rachel had visited. "It's all your counseling," she told Jack. "I told Karen how supportive you've been. She told me she'd heard of you and what a caring person you are many times. She said I couldn't have chosen a better person to coach me."

"Careful, Rachel. My head is swelling. But don't underrate your achievement--not to me, to Karen, or the manager. If you received a benefit from some of my experiences, don't forget it was you who asked the questions and you who put the answers to use. I appreciate your giving me a share of credit because credit is like a boomerang-- the more of it you pass around the more comes back to you. You've helped me too, you know. I really enjoy our conversations, not to mention the discussions on *Secrets of the Jungle*. Will you have time to take a look at the next chapter on reputation in the next few weeks?"

"I'll make time. I can't wait to get your ideas. You have a wonderful reputation."

That weekend, Paul and Brad were off on a camping weekend and Rachel began reading.

The Four Rings
Seven months had passed since I first met the Elder. I felt I had made a good decision to become a Healer and was feeling very comfortable in my Sorting role. Mali was there if I needed her, but I had no difficulty doing my work and often had time to help the others. I had been putting off my move to the Gatherers and was being pressed to make a decision.

So it was that early one morning the Elder asked me to walk with him. I knew he must have a reason, but each time I tried to ask him, he responded with a comment about the beauty of our surroundings. Finally, seated side by side near the top of a hill, we watched as the sun emerged from behind a cloud casting gold and pink ribbons across the sky. Then, he asked me a question. "Have you ever wondered what would happen if the sun refused to leave the shelter of the cloud?"

I was perplexed and a bit impatient. "That would never happen. It is natural for the sun to rise in the morning. It cannot stay where it is. It has no choice."

"Nor do you," he responded.

Now I understood. "I just don't feel ready to move. I would have to start all over again. Besides, I'm really good at sorting and I feel like an important member of the group. Nobody outside of the Sorters knows who I am and what I can do."

"Nor do you," he said once again. Then he added, "It is time to make a name for yourself."

"How do I do that?"

Picking up a stick, the Elder drew four circles on the ground, each within the other. He pointed to the outermost circle. "The first ring is to keep increasing your skills. When you become good enough that others seek your advice, the word will spread and others will hear of you."

"*But if I stop being a Sorter, then I won't be able to show my skills.*"

"*Believe in yourself. Others have seen that you know the roots, fungi, and berries from which we make medicines. Now you are ready to learn how to harvest them.*" *Then pointing to the next ring he said,* "*Just as the first ring is about what you do, the second ring is to show who you are by keeping to a high personal standard.*"

"*What does that mean?*"

"*There are those who wrap themselves in their own needs. They waste much time worrying about how each decision impacts them. They do not care what goes on in the Tribal Council unless they hear their names spoken. They feel no responsibility for the welfare of the tribe. If they do the sorting, they think gathering is unimportant. If they are traders, they cannot see the value of hunters. The only questions they ask or answer are those that affect them directly. They do not handle themselves well in meetings because they pout and sulk or even fight when others disagree.*"

"*What do people do who have a high standard?*"

"*They do not think about themselves but rather what is best for the tribe.*"

"*How can I ever....?*"

"*Keli, think back on all you have done already and you will believe in yourself as I believe in you. You learn quickly and you are self-disciplined. You do not waste the hours. You listen when others speak. You withhold angry words when you do not agree. There are other things you will learn in time, but they will come easily because you are a good person. Go to the tribal meetings. Watch how the Shaman and Wisemen act and do likewise. When people see you do these things, they will take note and your name will be honored.*"

"*I understand. Then what is the third ring?*"

"*How you treat others,*" *he said.* "*It is easy to be pleasant when things are going your way. It is harder when you must work with people who can be small and disagreeable. Just think before you confide in others. What you believe you said in private could become common knowledge, so do not say things you would not be proud to have repeated. Be kind, even when it is difficult. In the end, people remember how you treated them. When others speak of you, let it be for the way you care, whether it's the Tribal Chief or the smallest child."* Then the Elder pointed toward the center circle. *"This one is purpose. If you would make a place for yourself, you must have a purpose."*

"But what if I don't know my purpose? How can I find it?"

"You must be patient. Listen to your heart, examine your thoughts, and be guided by what they reveal. When you shoot an arrow, you know when it has found its mark. In the same way, when the time is right, you'll come to understand how you can best serve the Korios and find the core to your life's purpose. Remember this, the answer is within yourself, but it is not about yourself."

"Which of the rings is the most important," I wondered.

"They are all important," responded the Elder.

I knew he was right and that I would have to leave the safety and comfort of my group of friends to test myself and make my place. For a long time, neither of us spoke. This time I broke the silence and asked the Elder to tell me about his long service as a Healer. In this manner we passed the rest of the day. The Elder had held many different jobs and enjoyed every aspect of the work. We ate of the tender orange fruit of the hog plum tree as I listened to stories of the cures that had enabled many of my fellow tribesmen to lead long and productive lives. By the end of the day, I had made up my mind to make the change. As the sun set, both of us were aware of the significance it had for the two observing it--one near the beginning of the journey and one closer to the end. Then we rose and walked together down the hillside and toward the village.

■ ■ ■

"I'd like to talk about the circles," said the note in the middle of Jack's desk. "Give me a call if you have time for lunch today."

He did have time, and two hours later, seated by the window in the company cafeteria, Rachel and Jack were in the midst of a discussion.

"When I talk about demonstrating skill in the story, I'm basically talking about showing you have expertise regarding your work.

However, having technical skills means very little if no one is aware of them. You need to make them known. The trick is to do that without seeming to blow your own horn. Provide a report to the boss, offer to serve on a project team, give a short presentation at a meeting. Do something, but whatever you do, don't close your office door and do it in the dark."

"You mean the way I used to do it when I expected to be rewarded for hard work."

"Exactly. I found the second concept a bit more difficult to explain in the story, only because certain words and ideas don't fit with my jungle theme. Not that I haven't taken some liberties here and there," added Jack with a chuckle. "The idea I'm talking about is professionalism, which is a very broad term. It includes everything from the way you present your ideas to another group to how effectively you take charge of your time. It's handling yourself well in conflict situations or running a group meeting. It's considering things from the perspective of what's good for the team, or the company, rather than being self-absorbed. It's knowing how to say no – and doing it gracefully."

"I like the way you explain that as adhering to a higher standard of behavior."

"Well I hope it wasn't too much of a stretch. I might add some thoughts there if you think it necessary."

"I don't think so. I really did understand it, but how do you distinguish that from the third ring – how you treat others? Don't most business books put them together as interpersonal skills?"

"Some do. I see them as different. Let's say you have top-notch technical skills and are very good at resolving conflicts and presenting your ideas. But how other people respond to you also makes a big difference. Whether you call it interpersonal skill or likability, it impacts how quickly people return your calls and how eager they are to put you on their committee or project team. If you're the leader, it shows in the enthusiasm with which people follow you. It also determines the kind of information they share with you. Look, Rachel, if you had to choose between two equally qualified people to work with you, and one had a reputation for caring about people and the other didn't, who would you choose?"

"No contest. I'd go with the one who cared. Then if I had a problem, I'd have someone who would listen. Now let's go to the real reason I wanted to talk. That's the inside circle, the one you call *purpose*. I think I understand what you were talking about. It's knowing what you are trying to achieve, isn't it?"

"Yes, but it's more than that. It really answers the most important question: *why*. Without purpose everything you do is an activity. Some activities are successful, some aren't. You can have many different goals and feel very good about achieving them – but in support of what? That's what you have to consider."

"I mean, you're not talking about a higher purpose, are you, Jack?"

"Not in the religious or spiritual sense. I think that's very important but it's outside the scope of this book, although I do think your work life is an extension of other parts of your life. There are people who check their personal selves at the door when they walk into the building. This can create a conflict – one they may not be aware of. But in this book, I'm focusing my attention on what work is about. You see, Rachel, you are more likely to hit the target when you know what you're aiming at. And if you want to make a name for yourself it answers the question – what name?"

JOURNAL ENTRY EIGHT
To Survive: Make sure your contributions are visible.

To Succeed: Combine high standards of professionalism toward work with a caring behavior toward people.

To Shine: Choose how and for what you want to be remembered. That is your purpose in life. Your reputation is a product not only of what you do but also of who you are.

The Ninth Secret

On Getting Your Work Approved

"Attention is a precious commodity."

BRIAN SOLIS

One hand on her hip, and shaking her head in mock disgust, Rachel stood in the doorway to Jack's office. "You look entirely too rested to me. Here I was up to my eyebrows in pressure, running here, running there, tossing and turning every night while you and Laura were lying on gigantic beach towels in Maui sopping up the sand and the sea. I'll bet the worst pressure of the trip was deciding where to have dinner every night."

"Enough!" said Jack, laughing as he handed her a small package containing the necklace Laura had purchased for her at one of her afternoon expeditions. "Let me buy my way out of this."

Rachel smiled as she held up the double strand of pink seashells. "Thanks, Jack," she said. "Please thank Laura and tell her I love it."

"Okay. Your turn. Tell me what you've been up to."

He listened intently as Rachel told of the proposed new pricing system. She just completed the study she told him. As she concluded, she held up two crossed fingers. "So far, so good. But wish me luck!"

"This is great!" He told her. "This will give you a lot of visibility. You've earned it. And you don't need any luck."

"I wish I were as confident as you," responded Rachel with a sigh. "If work and effort would do it, we'd be home free. Right now the odds of approval are 50-50 at best."

"Who has to approve it?"

"Only the top level of our marketing managers: that's Alan Rankin, Terry Standish and Phyllis Colin. They can be tough Jack."

"Of course they can be, and they should be," he said. "Otherwise, good projects like yours would take a backseat as everyone pushed their own agendas. Will they support you?"

Rachel shrugged her shoulders. "I wish I knew."

"You need to get some idea before the meeting. We'll get back to that in a minute. If they like it, can they approve it?"

"I'm not sure, Jack. It may need to go to the Management Council."

"You need to know that before the meeting too. Making a formal proposal without knowing what kind of support you have and what obstacles you face is like going into battle without a shield or a sword. It is possible to survive anyway, but you wind up with more scars."

Rachel nodded. "I see what you mean," she said. "But how do I get that information?"

"Have I got a deal for you!"

"I'll bet it's Chapter Nine," she laughed. "Hand it over, and let's talk tomorrow. You've planted some seeds and I want to talk about how to grow them."

This time Rachel did not wait to go home. If Chapter 9 could help, she wanted to start on it immediately.

The Plan
Our group of Gatherers was dejected as we walked toward the village. We had spent three days searching for the golobe fungus without any luck. The medicines to cure infections were vital to the health of every villager, and

our supplies were running dangerously low. Tolar ran to meet us as we approached the village. When he saw our empty baskets, the disappointment we felt was reflected on his face. The Elder Healers must meet tomorrow at sunrise, he told us, to decide what to do. I had been thinking about this day and night as we searched the forest for the plants and wondered if we might trade one of the other tribes some skins, meat or medicine for the supplies to keep us going until we found the fungus.

Tolar thought about it for a moment. Then he nodded. "It would be good to go to the elders with a plan," he said. "Talk to other villagers today, Keli. The Traders and Hunters often run into tribes from the Valley or across the river. See if you can learn from them which tribes might be willing to help us and what we could trade. Then we could go to that meeting tomorrow and you could ask the Elder Healers about this."

I was excited and a little nervous about the prospect of being heard at such an important meeting. But who should I talk to? And what should I say? I went to see the Elder. We walked toward the river, and for a moment, he seemed lost in thought. Then he turned to me and said, "You proposed a good solution, Keli, and one the elders would be interested in hearing more about. It pleases me because you have the tribe's interest at heart and because Tolar has shown great confidence in you. What would you learn from me?"

"I'm not sure what I should do next. I know I could ask Tolar, but I'm afraid he will think I am not wise if I do."

"Ah, but you are wise. Those who are not, act without thinking. It is far wiser to admit you do not know and seek help than to act as if you know and thus fail to receive it." He paused for a moment, then added, "If you want the elders to listen when you speak, you must understand the ways to get their approval."

"What ways do you mean?" I asked.

"First, you must be sure of what you speak. Seek knowledge from those who've walked the same path so when you speak to the elders, they will see that you are wise."

"*How do I do that? Tolar told me to ask the Hunters and the Traders, but there's so little time. Who should I talk to? I know Pardo and Kodi. Both are Traders. Should I go to them?*"

"*No, for neither of them sits near the seat of power. You have met Tahu the elder. Because he sits close to the Chief Trader, he is a better choice. Now which of the Hunters do you know?*"

"*I could ask Bari. We have walked the path many times before we separated, he to go to the hunt, and I to gather medicine plants. He knows the Hunter Wiseman well, and he could help me.*"

"*Then he is a good choice. Also, when you wait to speak tomorrow, show the Elder Healers great respect. Sit patiently without speaking while we lay out our concerns. Then allow Tolar to speak before you. He will tell us you wish to speak, but you should remain silent. You must wait for all the Elders to acknowledge you first. Notice what words the Elders use and do not use when addressing one another. You will see that no one uses the word 'I' for we Elders disdain it. As you describe the plan, you must ask for our counsel. These are the ways that show the proper respect for experience, age and wisdom, and they are required of you.*"

"*Now tell me more about your plan,*" he continued. "*Who would we send to meet with these other tribes to work out a trade, or would you ask the elders to decide who should go?*"

"*There are others with greater wisdom who must make this decision. Will you support me in the meeting?*"

"*I will, Keli. It is also most important to know before the meeting if the other two Elder Healers will support you or if not, for what reasons they might oppose the trade, for then you can decide what you need to say to them. If they support you, you will want to spend most of the time describing the plan; if they do not, you must spend most of it showing how the tribe will benefit. By doing this, you will grow in the Elder Healers' eyes for you are showing respect for their time and the weight of the decision they bear.*"

"*But I thought the meeting was to get their support.*"

"Ah, my young friend, such meetings are rarely arranged to get support. Rather they are a necessary means of demonstrating that support you already have."

"Then how do I find out if they will support or oppose the trade?"

"There are several ways. The best way is to visit them after you have talked with Bari and Talu. If you do not feel you know them well enough or for some other reason cannot see them, you must find other sources that know them well, perhaps a friend who sits beside them as you do me. Perhaps Tolar. Use this information to prepare yourself for the meeting."

"You sit beside them in the meetings. What can you tell me?"

"Only this much: Cossi will wonder which Traders and Hunters you spoke with and what concerns they had; Balar will be most interested in the details of your plan."

I had no more questions. We walked back in silence. The closer we got to the village, the more my confidence grew. Thanks to the Elder, I had a plan, and when I spoke to the Elder Healers the next day, he would be there to support me.

∎∎∎

Rachel reread the last page of Chapter 9 as she waited for Jack. Walking briskly into his office, he was momentarily startled to find Rachel sitting at the small conference table near the open door. "Oops, sorry," he said. "The old boy was acting up again."

"No problem, " she laughed, knowing he was referring to his cherished 1939 Packard. "Just start his engine with coffee. That will get him going. It works for me. This is my second cup, and I'm shifting into third gear already. Anyway, I'm here to talk about *Secrets* and get your advice on my project."

Jack poured himself a cup of coffee and waited. "Reading the chapter made me realize why it's important to assess the territory before the meeting. I've already tapped into some sources to find out how much support I have on the Marketing Council. So far, so good.

Now here's what I'm wondering. You talk about observing the rules. How does that apply to my situation?"

"Rachel, if you want to be successful in any organization, you must learn the unspoken rules. That requires your understanding the way things are done. These unspoken rules or protocols lie deeply entrenched in every facet of the way any organization conducts its internal business. They underlie the way it communicates, how it dispenses information, and how it makes key decisions. Those who violate the protocols are rarely successful."

"Every organization has communication protocols," continued Jack. "This regards everything from who speaks to whom to the choice of words used in meetings or in any formal business situation. For example, before I came here, Reed and Connors, the company I worked for, had subjects and even words that were taboo. We never used them because management was highly sensitive to them and let us know it. Once I was in a meeting and heard someone describe a pilot project as a failure. You would not have believed the scowls and looks of disapproval. Her manager told her later to never use *that word* again. The pilot was not a failure, he told her. It was a learning experience with limited success."

Rachel giggled. "Limited success?"

"I'm serious," said Jack smiling. "Another protocol at R&C regarded questioning management decisions, particularly in a meeting. It just wasn't allowed. It was apparent that R&C managers regarded themselves as much smarter than their regular employees. While in some cases this could possibly be true, cutting off communication could prevent them from finding the best solutions."

Rachel shook her head. "I'm glad it is different in our company."

"Me too. Every organization is different but if you really want to be successful, you recognize its unspoken rules. Once you step beyond them, you may achieve results – but they are likely to be the wrong ones. Besides topics and words, another implicit rule of communication to watch for involves the direction it flows in the company. In open organizations, it moves up and down and sideways. In more closed organizations it tends to flow one way, down. At PWE, when management sends out an employee questionnaire, it openly discusses the results and involves employees in plans to work on problem areas. R&C sent out surveys yearly, but management carefully word-smithed the results and only occasionally involved employees in any plans."

Jack continued, "Now, based on what you learn about the protocol, you can begin to understand what management's attitude toward communication is, and this is very important. If management uses direct and honest communication with employees and encourages straight responses, then we can say its attitude is very open. That means, if you are in a meeting, it is okay to tactfully challenge someone's ideas. That's how it is here at PWE. At Reed, management's attitude was that communication was about achieving a specific result. Employees spent a great deal of time there rewording their presentations to management. Management, in turn, spent a good deal of time on the wording of its communications with employees."

"Doesn't that speak volumes about mutual trust?"

"It probably does. The important thing is when you meet with the Marketing Managers, you will need to be straightforward about the positives and negatives, if any, of your proposal."

"I have three questions," said Rachel. " First, you mentioned information and decision making as well as communication. Are those the only areas where protocols exist?"

"Not really," said Jack. "There are dress protocols, especially for headquarters. There are office appearance protocols as well, but the ones you mentioned are the most important. When it comes to information and decision making, rules can be particularly subtle. Take information for example. In some companies, everyone knows what is going on. In others, organizations hold information more tightly than the CIA. People are included on a need-to-know basis only. But what I am describing are the extremes. Most organizations, like ours, fall somewhere in between."

"So, from that you can figure out what management's attitude toward information is. In open organizations, management trusts employees to hear both good and bad news because it believes that knowledge enables everyone to be more productive. This is usually true of flatter organizations. In closed organizations, management withholds sensitive information because it fears that people won't be able to handle the truth for one reason or another. This is most typical in multi-layered organizations where people equate knowledge with power.

"Decision making protocols are exactly the same," continued Jack. "In open organizations, many decisions are made at the lowest levels feasible. The belief is that the people most closely involved in the work have the best information. In closed organizations, decision-making is generally the sole prerogative of managers. In those companies the feeling is that since information is not widely handed out, the workers are not in a position to know. Again, those are extremes. Most companies fall somewhere in between. The more bureaucratic a company is, the more it tends to push decisions, even the smallest ones, up. So, what was your second question?"

"If a company is closed in one area, as in sharing information, does it necessarily follow it will be closed in all three?"

"Well, it's a matter of degree. A company may be completely closed in the way it provides information but a bit more open in its communication to employees. At the same time, you can see how they would work hand in hand. A free flow of information generally encourages good communication. The more information people have, the more likely they are to make good suggestions. When that happens, organizations begin to see how helpful it is to get input from employees before making certain decisions. On the other hand, closed companies tend to be much more organized and far less sloppy than open companies."

"But are they as creative?" asked Rachel.

"Not really. However, sometimes creativity is not considered a high value. The important thing is, you need to understand the protocol or you will find yourself operating like a refuge from a closed system in an open one, or vice versa."

"Okay, Jack. Now for the grand prize, my third question. If you work in a more closed company, how do you communicate and get information? Also, how can you influence decisions?"

"I think that's two questions. On the first one, in closed companies, people observe the protocols in formal situations, but there are informal customs that apply as well. For example, at R&C, when people were in formal meetings, they never spoke of *problems*. In fact, we laughingly referred to that as "using the p-word." The real meetings happened after the formal meetings were over. Then people congregated in their offices, closed the doors, and interpreted what the events in the meeting meant. Sometimes, friendly managers would come and share insights informally with us. So, if you understand the protocol and the attitude in the closed environment, you use the informal system."

"Sounds like a lot of time is wasted in speculation," Rachel opined.

"The important thing is having a good network. If you don't have one, you're subject to hanging out with those who spend great amounts of time spreading idle rumors. The problem is rumors, like gossip, are like whirlpools. They suck you in, but there's neither light nor air down there. That's why people who live and work in closed organizations should avoid getting information that way or giving much credence to what they hear."

"I agree," said Rachel. "My friend who works for another company, a closed one for sure, tells me about lots of speculation and wild rumors that have never come true. She thinks they are based on wishful thinking."

Jack nodded. "The funny part of it is that people who spread the rumors or engage in speculation rarely know what's going on.

In fact, those who know the most usually say very little, at least for public consumption. Instead, it's wise to use your powers of observation and your understanding of the company's protocol and attitudes to learn what you need to know. Then turn to reliable networks to confirm the facts. Above all, avoid participating in rumors, gossip, or idle speculation. The mud they generate often adheres to you."

"I suppose there are rules that apply to decisions as well," said Rachel. "I have another friend who works in a closed environment. I wonder if she can influence decisions made by managers."

Jack smiled. "So, now you're mentoring your friends, eh? I like that. Decision making is related to organization charts and hierarchies. They determine how much authority and control is exercised by the top and what level of decision the employee at each level can make. The good news is that even in closed companies your friend can have influence. The secret goes back to what we talked about in creating a good reputation. There are people in every organization who are thought leaders. They may not have decision making power, but they are widely respected and consulted by those who do. When those people know who you are and what you stand for, they will seek you out."

"Like they do with you," said Rachel.

"Just like that. In formal systems, you're anointed. In informal systems, you earn your place and the right to be involved. One more thing, Rachel, and this is important. You have to be willing to put your stake in the ground. You have to show that there are things you believe in strongly enough to stand up and be counted."

"Isn't that risky? I mean if you take a strong stand, mightn't that affect your ability to influence decisions?"

"That's true. So you need to be thoughtful in the exercise of that, but if you want to have influence, people need to know you are willing to take that risk for what you believe. I have a friend in another organization who had a very strong belief that the company should provide laptop computers so employees could work at home if they needed to. He had to convince a very reluctant management, and he did it by persuading key thought leaders, who in turn got several managers to try this out. At the time, there was heated debate, but now everyone sees the value of it. Consequently, his influence has grown."

"I'm glad you can influence closed organizations," said Rachel, "but I think PWE is more open in its decision making, don't you think?"

"A bit," said Jack, knowing where this was leading.

"And yet," continued Rachel, "I've learned when it comes to the pricing project I'm involved in, the decision will probably be made by the Marketing managers followed by the endorsement of the Management Council. I guess that's a protocol, right?"

"You got it."

"So tell me, Jack, is Keli going to be successful in the meeting?"

"Of course, he is. Didn't he get good advice and act on it? And besides, in *Secrets* it's the author's prerogative to make everything come out right."

"Wish you were writing my story. Then I could be sure this project would be approved."

"What do you think so far?" asked Jack. "I know you've been checking on how much support you have from the Marketing Managers."

"Things look good. But then, I'm like Keli. I get good advice, and I follow it."

JOURNAL ENTRY NINE

To Survive: Learn the organization's unspoken rules-- its communication, information, and decision making protocols.

To Succeed: Use your network to tap into the informal system.

To Shine: Build influence by being willing to put your stake in the ground.

The Tenth Secret

On Major Changes and Upheavals

"It does not do to leave a live dragon out of your calculations, if you live near him."

J.R.R. Tolkien *The Hobbit*

It was like being in the midst of a thunderstorm. Rumors of reorganization swept through the company like lightning bolts. Talk of layoffs echoed like distant thunder. People were anxious. They saw managers scurrying to meetings behind closed doors. After the meetings, they heard nothing. It was rumored they were there to determine the fate of departments, field units and even individual employees. Telltale signs of concern were the frequent small gatherings in many offices. Doors were shut and conversations were in whispers.

Behind one of the doors on the eighth floor, Rachel paced as she told Jack what she had heard. Then with a sigh, she dropped down into a handy chair – and waited.

Several moments passed before Jack spoke. "Okay," he said, "so you've heard there's going to be a reorganization. You're not sure if it's to be the whole company or specific departments – but you hear the company will reduce layers of management and downsize and whole areas will be outsourced. Does that sum it up?"

"Pretty much," she replied. "Jack, I don't like this and I feel helpless. I don't know what to do."

"And you came to me because...."

"Because I don't know how much of it is true, and you always know what's going on."

"How much of what you've told me is rumor and what part of it, if any, is fact?"

"I've gotten it from my network, more or less. Admittedly it's mostly rumor – but my sources (who shall remain anonymous, per instructions from you) are in different departments and the rumors are too similar to be discounted."

"Rachel, that doesn't prove anything. There's one thing you can be sure of – if the rumor is exciting, the informal network, or grapevine, will move it as fast as the speed of sound. To be fair, I've got the sense that change is in the works too. In fact, I've been writing about it in Chapter 10, which I am going to give you to read. Give me a few days to find out what I can. I'll call you when I have more info. In the meantime, my best advice is to be cool and that means try to stay away from the small clusters of people hanging out in offices trading rumors. No matter what changes are made eventually, there is still work to be done. Don't seek out more answers yet, and above all, don't contribute to the misinformation that's floating around."

Rachel felt better. She reached for Chapter 10, promising to await Jack's call. As she walked out, she paused in the doorway to his office. "When we talk, will you tell me how you figured out change is in the works? I'm wondering if you heard rumors too or are there other ways?"

"I will," said Jack. "And you're right there are other ways – more reliable than rumors. Think of them as drumbeats. I'll call."

That night Rachel started reading.

The Storm
A storm was brewing. Even before the thunder intensified, even before the clouds darkened, I could sense it was different from the typical jungle storms--and far more menacing.

Shine

First were the days when the faint echoes of thunder vibrated like drumbeats from afar. They were followed by nights with no breeze at all when a pervasive stillness hung in the air. The birds, insects and animals of the jungle seemed to know of the approaching storm long before the thunder and lightning threatened the village. All the normal jungle sounds, the hoarse brr of the tanagers, the staccato shriek of parakeets, the shrill hum of the beetles, the screeching of the spider monkeys increased in volume and intensity. The rustling in the trees and on the ground signaled a restlessness and movement that I could feel in every part my body.

When the storm hit, I was awed by its ferocity. First came the lightning – in flashes of energy that seemed to pierce the skies and create an eerie glow over the village. It was followed by the thunder rising from a faint rumble to a deafening roar that seemed to shake the earth beneath my feet. I wanted to move, to run – but I was transfixed by the sheer power of the storm. A crackling sound followed by loud cries jolted me from this trance-like state. It was fire – the village was in flames. Silhouettes appeared in the darkness as villagers hurriedly gathered possessions and raced toward the river. "Keli, Keli--hurry!" It was Mali, but I hung back.

"The Elder--where's the Elder?"

"Over there," she said, pointing toward the clearing. He sent me to get you."

He was directing excited villagers toward the hill and away from the river, sending others with messages to the Chiefs and Wisemen when Mali and I reached his side. "Carry these," he said, gesturing toward baskets of foliage, "and run to the hill."

"But what about you?" I protested. He was already engaged in animated conversation with Pola, and I could see he would pay me no more attention. So we ran, Mali and I, with baskets of healing plants and berries in our arms toward the hill. That night we returned many times, too many to count, to salvage other precious supplies. Then came the dawn when exhausted, we lay down at the edge of the hill.

Our sleep was short and disturbed by drops of rain – at first gentle, then increasingly persistent. Tired and soaked, we sought shelter beneath the canopy of trees surrounding the remains of the village and surveyed the scene. The fire was out, but most of the village had been reduced to smoldering heaps of ashes. Around the remains stood disconsolate groups of villagers – some talking, some weeping, other sifting through the ashes in search of some special treasure left behind.

We saw a group of Healers and hurried to join them. "What's going on?" I asked. "What are we going to do?"

"We're going to rebuild the village right here," said a young Sorter.

"No, no," said one of the Gatherers. "The Tribal Council and the Elders are meeting right now to decide where to go."

"Some of us will be moved to other villages," said a third Healer. "We don't know whether we will go or stay. Maybe some of us will have to go to another place."

I felt myself becoming anxious as we stood there talking in the ruins of the village. Mali must have sensed how I was feeling. "Let's go, Keli," she said. "We will look for Pola. She usually knows before anyone what the Tribal Council is planning."

As we walked toward the pond, Mali stopped suddenly. "There! Look there!" she said, pointing to the clearing on the other side of the water. I saw the village Elders, the Wisemen, and the Chiefs huddled together. Pola was sitting beside the pond not far from the Tribal Council. She motioned for us to join her. Her smile was a warm and welcome contrast to the dismal and depressing atmosphere we had just left.

"There are all kinds of stories being told out there, Pola," I said. "But which of them is true? One person said we will rebuild the village right here. Someone else thought the whole tribe might have to move away. Then I heard we might even be asked to stay with another tribe. I don't know what to think. I'm worried." Mali nodded her agreement.

Pola listened intently. Finally she took my hand and Mali's and said, "I don't want you to worry about this. The Tribal Council and Elders are wise. They've been through many misfortunes and they know what to do. They have been meeting through the night and all of the morning debating and discussing many different options. Soon they will call us together to tell us what has been decided. One thing the Elder told me early this morning – it is likely that some of us will stay here and rebuild the village. The rest will probably go to our small northern village."

I felt better because I trusted Pola and now had more information. I thought about the other Healers and how knowing this might help them too. "You want me to go back and tell the others?" I asked.

Pola thought for a minute. Then she responded, "That's a good idea, but let's wait a little while. I want to find out if there will be any big changes in this plan first. We won't wait long though. If the Tribal Council is not finished by the time the moonbeams near the Hill, we will tell the others what we know."

"How will the Council decide who goes and who stays?" asked Mali. "Will we have a choice?"

"I'm not sure," said Pola. "What is most likely – and don't depend on this – is that some of our leaders will go and some will stay. Some of the tribe will be asked to stay or go based on need and others will be able to volunteer. But that's just my guess."

"I hope the three of us stay together," said Mali. "I don't mind going or staying, but I don't want to lose my friends."

"What would happen if we three volunteered to go? Could we do that?" I wondered.

Pola nodded. "Maybe we could. But I think we should consider the good of the village first. Let's see where they need the most help. Then the three of us can volunteer for that, whatever that is."

"What if the Tribal Council has already decided?" asked Mali. "Do you think we can get them to change their minds?"

"They are great leaders. They are also very wise," said Pola. "If there is a way they can accommodate our needs, they will surely do that. Perhaps we should approach the Elder. He will help us if he can."

Mali stayed with Pola and I returned to the hillside to sort through the baskets. There would be time enough for plans later. Now we needed to know what remained of our store of healing material. It appeared that we had salvaged a good supply of pokeweed berries, ipoh roots and konoyah leaves, enough to last for several months.

When I went back to give Pola and Mali the good news, I was greeted by two sad faces. The Elder was leaving. He would be gone for many months journeying through the jungle gathering supplies from other tribes to replace those we lost in the fire. I was stunned. I depended on him for so much, and I loved him like a father. "Perhaps he will take me with him," I said. "I'll talk to him. It will be all right."

I felt Pola's arm around my shoulder. "It is not to be, Keli. The Wisemen have decided. There is much to be done here. You are young and strong. We need you to help rebuild the village. Your knowledge and skills have been recognized. You are to become the head Gatherer."

"But I could talk to them," I said. "He cannot go alone. He needs someone young like me to help him."

"He will be traveling with three Hunters and two Traders. It is decided."

I was bereft.

■ ■ ■

"I know how Keli feels," said Rachel as she stepped inside Jack's office, closing the door behind her. "We'll be losing some people if there is a downsizing, and it's going to hurt."

"Of course it will."

"Okay, Jack. You said you have some news. Shoot!"

"There will be a downsizing. My sources say it should be announced in just two weeks. I hear PWE management will be reduced to three layers."

"What about the rest of us?"

"The best number I could get was six to seven percent will go."

Rachel groaned. "That's more than one hundred people."

"I know."

"So what are the chances it could happen to me?"

"Rachel, no one can know for sure at this point. I think they are small. You are respected in both HR and Marketing. See the Healers and Traders both like you," he added with a grin.

"That's not funny," she said, trying to hide a slight smile. "All right, Jack, so I'd make it in the jungle."

"You're in the jungle now."

"So, how do people survive times like these--with everything spinning around. I don't like change. It always comes along just when you're getting comfortable."

"Over the years I have learned there are certain steps to doing well in a rapidly changing environment. And I'll save you the trouble of asking what they are.

"Step One is to gather information. Most important is to pick up that info from people who would be most likely to know."

Rachel nodded. "Another reason to have a good network."

"Right. There will always be rumors, gossip, and some interesting signals, if you can read them."

"Are those the drumbeats you spoke of earlier?"

"They are. For example: there are a lot of clues from the external environment that change is afoot. That's one extra reason to read business journals as well as the business pages of a reliable newspaper. If reorganizations, buyouts or outsourcings are happening in other companies within the industry, it is a pretty good indication that we will experience similar changes before long. After all, the same market issues and economic circumstances apply to all of us. So look for industry trends, economic indicators and the like.

"The internal clues are there as well – but they're often harder to read. Some things I have noticed in our company: before there is any major change announced, there are usually management speeches about how we must do something about staffing or productivity – and we need to be thinking about how we're going to get to the next milestone. Then there is usually a flurry of meetings at higher levels. Often these are off-site. In fact, you'll see some rather strange combinations of managers going – that is, people who rarely attend the same meeting. Sometimes a new training program, one that deals with work processes (like reengineering), is announced.

People are selected to be trained, or everyone is lined up for the classes. Occasionally there are consultants, more than usual, brought in. Some of these people specialize in worker productivity, reorganization or outsourcing. During this period, if you ask for information, you are likely to get less than usual. Don't spend too much time worrying about it. Just begin to look for answers."

"All I feel in this situation is helpless."

"But you needn't be, Rachel. Once you begin to form some idea about what is happening, talk with a couple of key people in your network. Tell them what you suspect. Ask them if they have heard anything they can share in confidence. If they haven't heard, they will usually tell you, but don't think that means it won't happen. If you have developed relationships built on trust and confidence, you'll get information in some form. The most important thing to remember is to focus on what you can control.

"So, let's move on to Step Two. That's an important mental process called Anticipating. It's messy, but crucial. You ask yourself, 'What will happen if....? What's the worst thing that could happen? What's the likelihood of it happening? How would it affect the business? How would it affect me?'"

"But Jack, if you don't know for sure, how would that help?"

"Look, people are always anxious in a time of change. But sometimes, if you think about things, you realize there is little reason for your anxiety. But let's take the worst case. Suppose there is reason to be anxious. Sitting around and waiting--or worse, building your anxiety by compounding it with that of others, won't help. The universal balm is action. So think of anticipating as a way to get started. And that brings me to Step Three: action planning.

"Start by considering things you can do to influence the outcome. This might include talking with your supervisor about a move or temporary assignment into another part of the company. It could also involve calling people in your network and letting them know you are looking for an opportunity. Find out what is going on in their areas. Someone who has mentored you might be a good resource at this point. No matter what the outcome is, don't panic. What you are doing is quietly assessing your options.

"Next, prepare for the possibility of a job search by updating your resume and contacting your external network. This is a good time to gather financial data--to consider how you would manage this important aspect of your life in case of a job search. Alert family members to the potential situation and enlist their support.

"Third, it won't hurt to circulate your resume through your external network--and beyond. You might also do a little research as you consider what placement agencies might be viable sources for you. At this point you need to do some serious thinking about your priorities and your career. What do you really want? Have your priorities changed? Maybe you planned to stay with one company, but now you see an opportunity to do something else. Do you want to go back to school? Stay home? Start your own business? What is most important to you in making a career decision? What are the most important ingredients you would like to see in a new position? Make sure you include the opportunities to grow in knowledge and skills. Differentiate between needs and wants. Would you be interested--or willing--to relocate? To consider related fields? These are the critical questions you must answer as you develop your plan.

"Now, with an action plan in hand, continue to do the high quality work you're getting paid for. In periods of change, people sometimes focus so much attention on their fears that little gets done. Be supportive to your friends, but remember--you are still on the payroll. That's not just being loyal to the company. It's also being loyal to being the professional you are. Be sure to keep your own counsel about your plans. By taking these steps, you will have increased your sense of control and reduced your anxiety level.

"Step Four is to stay alert to possibilities and opportunities. Continue to gather data by keeping your eyes and ears open. Stay in touch with those network members who have shown a willingness to help. Go back to Step Three, if you see a reason to adjust your action plan.

"Step Five: If necessary, execute those parts of your plan that are not already activated. You've got the framework. You've considered the contingencies. You've determined how to finance it. Now all you have to do is ACT!

Step Six is Evaluate and Readjust. Let's suppose that you turned out not to be personally affected by the changes. That is, you're still here, your job may have changed some but it's roughly equivalent to what you were doing before, or perhaps you've been moved to a different job. Never believe that once it's over, it can't happen again. It can--and it probably will. You need to evaluate the process you just went through to see if your networking and strategy were effective or if some changes are required. Make needed adjustments and rest in the security that you have greater control of your own destiny.

"Suppose you left the company, either because of the downsizing or by choice. Then you still may need to evaluate and readjust in your new line of work. It's hard to find a company of any size where changes aren't happening."

Rachel had listened intently. She could see the value of all that Jack had explained, but her initial response was emotional. She sighed, "I'd be hurt if that happened to me."

Jack nodded. "That's understandable," he said. "It's okay to feel angry or hurt for awhile--but remember, the best remedy is action. Should you plan to update your skills? Gain others? Retrofit yourself for a new occupation? This is an interesting playing field. Don't be a spectator."

"I know you're right, and that's great advice. So what's going to happen to Keli--and the village?"

"The Elder will be gone for some time, but Keli and Pola and the others will rebuild the village, and --because of the challenge, they will grow in ability and inner strength. That's what challenges do for us."

"I guess they are some of the tests you spoke of a long time ago."

"They are, Rachel."

"What's the next chapter about?"

"It's about the rain forest and balance and interdependence."

"Do you have it yet?"

"I still have to finish it, but here, take the first part and by the time you've finished it, I'll probably have the rest."

"That's a deal!"

JOURNAL ENTRY TEN

To Survive: Assess the potential effect of the change and develop a plan.

To Succeed: Consider alternatives, develop a strategy, and take early action.

To Shine: Influence the outcome and its impact on you using your internal and external networks for information, support, and help.

The Eleventh Secret

On Community

"I know there is strength in the differences between us. I know there is comfort where we overlap."

Ani DiFranco

The reorganization was over. Some people – good people – were gone. Goodbyes had been said. Some were tearful; some, joyful; others full of excitement and hope. The new organization had been announced and people poured over the charts looking for their names and the names of their friends. Jack had a new role as Senior Advisor to the president on employee issues. Bill had opted for an early retirement package, and Rachel had just told Jack about her promotion to team leader in the company's Wholesale Marketing Division.

"I don't know whether to laugh or cry," she said. "I guess I'd better put on my best face for the new senior advisor. An office next to the president – I'm impressed."

"Frankly, I'll miss it down here on eight. And we'll have a bit of a walk now that you're moving into the Marketing Center. Good exercise for both of us," he grinned. "Have you met with your new team yet?"

"No, but I've heard a few things from their last team leader. It should present an interesting challenge."

"Is there friction?"

"No Jack, nothing as visible as that. From what I hear, it's more like a dysfunctional family, with people going their separate ways. My understanding is – I think it may be a diversity issue – but I'm hesitant to say that until I see for myself."

"Good idea not to make any hasty evaluations. PWE and Marketing have made a great choice in you. Have you started reading Chapter 11 yet?"

"I'm embarrassed, but no. If you give me the rest of the chapter, I do have time now."

"Here's a new version," he said reaching into his briefcase. "I've done some serious editing since I gave you the first part. Anyway, I think you'll find it interesting, particularly in view of the challenges you're facing."

She paused at the door, "I'll read it over the weekend. I hope there's some good advice in here, Jack. I have a hunch I'll be needing it."

Saturday afternoon was unusually quiet. Rachel had used all her powers of persuasion to get Paul and Brad to run her usual weekend errands so she could curl up on the sofa and read. She would pay with an extra dose of Sunday afternoon football, he told her. As she picked up the manuscript, she made a mental note to do the wash on Sunday.

The Richness of Diversity
Our group of Gatherers had just returned from a successful five-day expedition with baskets full of masoesa bush leaves used for cleaning wounds and shemane fern for aching feet. I was looking forward to a few hours of rest and something to eat other than the manioc bread that was a staple on our travels through the jungle. I stopped by the cooking house and helped myself to one of the delicious yams roasting on the fire. There I heard the good news. Bari, one of the Hunters traveling with the Elder, had returned

to the village bringing cotton hammocks to replace those lost in the fire. He would be leaving the next morning, so I knew there wasn't much time if I wanted to talk with him. I did not want to miss this opportunity for he had news of the Elder. I found him sitting by the pond with Barto, who was now a Hunter, and had remained in the village.

When he left the Elder and the others, Bari told us, they were staying with the tribe of Kupas where they had managed to make some very good trades. He had sent a special hammock back for me. I was elated – first because the Elder was well and enjoying his travels through the jungle, and second, because I would once again enjoy the comfort of my hammock at night.

There was other news as well. Bari had been accompanied to the village by two Panjus, the only survivors of a tribal war. The Elder had befriended them in the jungle where they had shared their provisions and given him items he was able to trade with the Kupas. He had sent them with Bari to become part of our community. The one named Koni was supposed to be expert with the bow and arrow, so he would join the Hunters. The other, Jaro, had worked closely with the Panju Shaman, and the Elder had sent word that he could be a big help to the Healers.

I was not sure how the others would feel about adding a stranger to our group, but I was full of gratitude towards the Elder and decided to do everything in my power to make him welcome. "Where are the Panjus?" I asked. Barto grinned and pointed toward the river.

"Why do you smile?" I asked.

"See for yourself," he snickered

They were sitting on the riverbank when I first saw them. Even from a distance I could see them looking at me as if I were an unwelcome guest. I raised my hand in greeting. "I am Keli," I said.

They stood up, side-by-side, and I was taken aback by the strangeness of their appearance. They were very tall and had feathers in their earlobes and through their noses as well as strange markings that resembled the caracara hawk painted on their chests. The larger of the two had a string of beads suspended from his lower lip. Their hair was long and coated with a substance *that made it glisten in the sunlight. They wore old-fashioned breech cloths of a type no longer used by our tribe. As I approached, the larger one greeted me. "The Elder spoke of you," he said. "I am Koni, the Hunter."*

Then the other spoke, "I am Jaro," he said. "I do not shoot the bow and arrow as well as my brother. I do know many roots, leaves, and berries. I will work with you and the Healers if they will have me."

For a moment, I hesitated. Then swallowing deeply, I nodded. I wanted to do it – but the others? Then I turned to Koni. "Where do you sleep?" I asked him.

"There," he said, pointing to a makeshift hut behind some trees about 60 yards from the village. "Come, you will see."

As the three of us walked toward their dwelling, I was struck by how differently we lived. Our huts consisted of light rafters of small palms supported by trunks of forest trees. The roofs were thatched with large leaves neatly arranged and bound to the structure with forest creepers. All our huts were clustered together to form a circle with the chief's hut in the middle. This dwelling was off by itself. Sticks resting on stilts constituted its main structure. Its roof was made of several palm leaves placed together in a crisscross pattern. A jaguar skin hung across the doorway. Once inside I was even more amazed by how they slept. Instead of the soft swaying hammocks we were used to, they slept on wooden racks.

"Are these comfortable?" I asked.

Both brothers grinned. "When we are tired, we sleep," Jaro responded.

As I returned to the village, I wondered how or if these strangers would fit into our tribe. Pola, Manu, Mali, Barto and I talked about that on our evening walk.

"I don't know how I feel about their being here," said Mali. "They look so fierce with those feathers through their noses and beads hanging from their lips."

"I don't think the Panjus want to fit in," said Manu. "They live away from the village, and they even eat by themselves. I'm glad they don't walk the path of the Traders." Manu was now a Trader and had recently returned from the northern village.

"Did you see their hut?" asked Mali. "It looks strange. And Keli says they sleep on wooden beds." She shook her head in disbelief.

"This Koni--I heard his arrows never miss," said Manu, "and that he can hit a hummingbird in the eye at a distance from here to the river. How do we know they won't get up in the night and attack us? The rest of the Panjus died in a tribal war. We are a peaceful people."

"Wait a minute," said Pola. She had stopped walking and was shaking her head in disapproval. "First of all, the Elder sent Koni and Jaro to live with us. That speaks well for them. In the second place, Manu, since you will be meeting many different people as a Trader, I would think you could learn a lot from Koni and Jaro."

"Yes," said Barto. "And don't forget how much they helped us in the jungle. Without their provisions and trading items, the Elder would not have been able to send back the supplies so quickly."

"Perhaps all will be well," I added. "They seem friendly and eager to be accepted. We can teach them to be more like us. If they give up the breech cloths for our loose-fitting trousers, remove the feathers, cut their hair and....."

"Hold on!" said Pola. "Koni and Jaro are the last survivors of the Panjus. It is right that they should hold to their culture. Perhaps they will teach us about it so we can properly honor them. In our turn, we will teach them about the Korios, but we should not ask or expect them to take on our ways."

"But how will the Panjus adapt to our customs?" I asked.

"That is for Koni and Jaro to determine," answered Pola. "Let us agree that when we speak of either of the brothers that we will not call them the Panjus, which tends to create distance, but rather by the names given them by their parents--which is what we prefer to be called."

I agreed. "That is the respectful thing to do," I said.

"Yes, Keli, and being respectful is only the beginning. No one knows better than you what it feels like to be an outsider. We must include them. Manu, you said that they eat by themselves. If that is their choice, so be it. But I think we have all missed the opportunity to make them welcome by not inviting them to eat with us and walk with us."

"Do we have to?" asked Mali. "What if we don't want to be with strangers?"

"We must not forget, they are part of us now. And we have much to learn from them," said Pola.

"Okay," said Manu. "I'm going to try to make friends with them, but they're going to have to try to fit in."

"Wait a minute, Manu," I said. "Let's not test our new friends to see if they deserve our friendship. Jaro worked side by side with the Panju Shaman. That's enough for me. I'll bet he knows some medicines that we have never used."

"I'm going to get some pointers from Koni," said Barto. "I have seen how good he is with a bow and arrow.

In this way, our conversation turned from the fearful, negative view of the Panjus to curiosity and interest in two new members of the tribe, Koni and Jaro. More challenges lay ahead, but we had crossed the first bridge.

"I wish it were that easy to resolve differences," said Rachel, taking another sip of Sprite. She and Jack were sitting in soft blue easy chairs in his new office. "One discussion and all is well."

"I take that as constructive criticism," responded Jack. "You're right. Keli and his friends have made the first step when they decided not to 'raise the bar,' that is, not to make accepting Koni and Jaro conditional on their conforming to a set of artificial requirements. That's like creating a whole new set of rules for a game in progress. Still, they have a long way to go."

"You made some interesting points, Jack. I laughed when I read about Keli suggesting that the brothers should give up their feathers and beads in order to be assimilated into the tribe. Then I realized how important it is to differentiate between *dress codes* and *traditions*."

"That's right. When it comes to dress codes, every organization has expectations about how its personnel will look and dress. Those are thought of as reasonable standards, though some will dispute even that. Eliminating diversity is another thing entirely. That's about attempting to erase traditions and culture in the name of assimilation. Even our military has come to recognize the difference and altered their rules accordingly. What organizations have to be mindful of is that certain requirements put those who are culturally different at a disadvantage. It's sort of like starting a marathon one mile behind everyone else."

Rachel leaned forward. "Jack, one thing really struck home-- when Pola and the others decided to stop referring to the brothers as the Panjus in favor of using their names instead. As I've gone around talking to the members of the team, there have been numerous comments about 'the Asian.' In fact, T. L. Chin is Taiwanese and clearly doesn't appreciate being lumped with all Asians, as if there's no difference between his culture and that of The People's Republic of China, Japan, or Vietnam."

"Can you blame him?" asked Jack. "Don't we, as Americans, see ourselves as quite different from the French or the Germans?"

"Right! and they from us." said Rachel. "And calling others by their names, rather than by referring to them as part of a group, as Keli says, gives them the respect they deserve."

"So tell me about the comments you're hearing."

"Well, the team was kept pretty well intact after the downsizing, so T.L. is the only new person in the group. I've interviewed each of them separately to see what's on their minds. Let me summarize. They say it used to be fun in the team until T.L. showed up. They say he's a workaholic, standoffish, reserved, slow to act, doesn't mix with the others, and has no sense of humor. Need I go on?"

"Please don't," replied Jack, wrinkling his brows. "And what does T.L. say?"

"At first, darn little. Finally I got at it a bit by asking him what his experience as a team member has been like so far."

"And...."

"He sees the team as very cohesive, but he doesn't regard himself as a member of it. He says they make fast decisions without thinking them through and are unwilling to listen. He says he feels tested every single day and that it robs him of energy. And finally, he told me the team does not understand people from Taiwan. Apparently, the first day he came on they decided they would all have dinner together and go out. Without even asking his preference, they went to their favorite barbecue place. T.L. doesn't eat barbecue. That's not cultural so much as a personal preference. Then they dragged him to a football game. He doesn't enjoy football either."

"Neither do you. So much for starting off on the right foot."

"But I give them some credit. They were well-intentioned."

"I wonder how we would feel arriving in a foreign country only to be treated to a dinner of jellyfish and conversation replete with jokes that make no sense to us," said Jack. "And, oh by the way, let's complete the picture with a long evening of ritualistic theater that we don't understand."

Rachel nodded in agreement. "I know people who travel all over the world, and wind up hanging out with other Americans eating hamburgers and fries. But enough of that. I do have some ideas that I'd like to try on you, Jack. They're not the answer, but perhaps they are a start."

"I can't wait to hear what you're planning."

"Good, because they include some help from you, not in your official role but as the best mentor anyone could have."

"Watch it, Rachel. When I get that big a compliment, I usually reach in my back pocket and grab hold of my billfold. Seriously, how can I help?"

"My plan has three parts: first, I think our group is going to need some teambuilding, and part of that is going to be for each of us to share some things about the history, style, and cultural background that have gone into making us unique. I thought we might develop a listing of all our competencies and talents so we can appreciate the gifts each of us brings and call upon each other for help. How's that for a start?'

"I like that. You're not singling T.L. out but opening the group to disclosing the kind of information that will draw them closer together."

"I think it could help. I'm going to bring in a friend, Charley Jackson, to facilitate the session and help us with the second part: diversity training. Now comes the third part, and if you're willing, you have a role in this."

"You know I'll help if I can," replied Jack.

"I'd like to give T.L. a copy of your manuscript to read. I want to use it as a coaching tool. He's sharp, and he has some special gifts. He's the only one in the group with a background in international finance. As PWE goes global, we'll need a lot of help working with foreign currency. I don't think we've begun to tap into his expertise. Once the group gets past this hurdle and becomes a team again, and that means that everyone is seen as a contributing member, I think he can teach us all a lot. I know you're busy, but would you be willing to talk with him if he has any questions – I mean after he's read it. When I think of how much your book has helped me – what do you say?"

"Sure thing," Jack replied. I'll get you another copy right away. Anything else I can do?"

Rachel paused and took a deep breath. "Have you got a couple of minutes more?" she asked.

Glancing at his watch, Jack nodded "I'm in good shape for the next twenty minutes or so."

She stood at the window staring at the sky line for a moment, then turned toward him. "Jack, I'm feeling a bit overwhelmed. I'm not sure I can do a good enough job coaching him to make a difference."

"Full of self-doubts?"

"Yes."

"Do you mind if I ask you a personal question?"

"No."

"Have you ever felt discriminated against?"

She nodded as she once again sank down into the chair. "I guess so."

"Do you mind talking about it?"

"Unofficially, Jack, sometimes it's been subtle; sometimes it's been pretty obvious. I've had discounting remarks made to me and heard them made about others in my presence. Sometimes they were made in a joking manner; sometimes I felt that was a serious edge underneath them. I remember going into several meetings with Karen. One of the men made a comment, saying 'There's Karen and her little shadow.' What a put-down, to be reduced to being a child! I've never heard those kinds of comments made to men who attended a meeting together."

"What did you do?"

"Karen and I walked over to him and in a quiet, but commanding voice, she said, "Excuse me, were you talking about Rachel and me?' He sort of weaseled out. 'I was only joking. I didn't mean anything by it.' You know the scene. Then she said, 'Have you met Rachel? She's our top performer in Wholesale.' I love the way she handled that, but isn't it a shame you have to confront such things?"

Jack nodded. Rachel continued, "Once I was told that the reason I wasn't asked to be part of a larger meeting was it was a 'men only' session. Now I have no problem with men gathering with other men. I enjoy the company of women too, but that was a business meeting."

Jack frowned. "Dinosaurs," he said.

Rachel sighed. "Some of the dinosaurs were around thirty."

"They come in all ages," he said, shaking his head.

"One more thing, Jack. Sometimes discrimination isn't that overt. It's not so much what does happen as what doesn't. A case in point: Karen was the best supervisor I've had. She was much smarter and more skilled than any of the managers they brought in over her. I honestly believe she would have been the manager if she'd been a man."

"Why do you say that?"

"I'm not sure, Jack. It's just that the people they brought in spent half their time in her office, seeking her opinion. She came up with all the ideas; they made all the presentations. You tell me."

"Maybe that's one I can look into," said Jack. "What's her full name?"

"Too late. She took the program. Now she's gotten a great job at Fulmark. That's a loss for PWE."

"Rachel, just a few minutes ago you told me you were worried about coaching T.L. You have nothing to fear. You have a wealth of knowledge and you understand the pain."

"I know, but can I really help him enough?"

"You can, and you will. It's really to your advantage to pull this off. In the world we're living in with a global marketplace, being able to leverage off the talents of everyone is an essential skill. None of us have a monopoly on good ideas. Think of how much you, the team, and ultimately the company can learn from a different perspective. Speaking of that, you said there were three steps you plan to take. Add one more to your list--enabling."

"Which means....?"

"Let's suppose building a network is one of the areas you plan to coach T.L. in. Don't forget that opportunities have to be available. No one can do it sitting in an office, yours or his. Sometimes it helps to listen, sometimes to advise, sometimes to encourage, but more than anything it helps to find the right occasions so that T.L. can use the coaching."

"I need to do that with everyone, don't I?"

"You got it. What do you think are some specific areas where coaching could help?"

" There's networking. I know he has close friends who are Taiwanese, and that's great, but he needs to expand his network. I want him to get more recognition for what he contributes. Then there is a more sensitive subject. When I interviewed him, I got the impression that he attributes all issues between him and the team to his being Asian. Many of them really are but some are typical team disagreements and some are just different business judgments. I'd like to help him focus on doing something about those. I know how easy it is to attribute everything to ethnicity or gender. As a woman, I've fallen into that trap before. The problem is it shuts you off from any good feedback and everyone walks on egg shells trying not to offend you which prevents you from growing."

'That's it!" Jack responded. "The team needs to develop a more open and positive communication atmosphere, and you need to set the example."

"Ouch, Jack. You hit a nerve. That's why I'm so overwhelmed. I have no problem giving the others feedback. I hesitate to give it to T.L. because I don't want to offend him."

"I understand, but Rachel, you're good at that. Just keep it balanced."

"Balanced?"

"Yes. Be sure to tell the team what they are doing right. If you have trouble with that, then how can you tell them how to improve? Second, don't believe that giving feedback is your sole prerogative. If the team is to become more effective, they all need to take responsibility for feedback."

"I know, but that's not where we are now--not by a long shot."

"You have to start somewhere. Hopefully, the teambuilding and diversity sessions you are planning will open the door to good constructive communication." Jack continued, "Let me share with you an experience that could throw some light on why I feel so strongly about straight feedback. Years ago I met June, a young African-American who was interning with PWE. She had been assigned to write a report which involved collecting information from me and others. Everyone of us found her manner abrasive. Because I didn't know her very well, I thought her supervisor could help her. When I suggested to Morgan that she might want to coach June or send her to some interpersonal skills training, she acted surprised, saying no one had been critical of June before. Instead of working with her, which I believe was her obligation, she asked me to talk to June. It was awkward because I barely knew her, but I thought she needed to know how she was coming across. Anyway, June was grateful. I think it was too late for her with PWE. She didn't receive a job offer, and I'll always wonder if Morgan was at least partially to blame. After she left, several others told me they also had spoken to her about June, even before I did. It was a real loss for PWE. June was bright, creative, and had a lot of initiative. We failed her."

"And I'm not going to fail T.L."

"Of course you're not. So, do you mind if I suggest six secrets to share with him?"

"I've got my pencil out."

"Here is what you should tell him. First, seek feedback, because it's information that will help you grow. If all you hear is positive, keep probing. We are all imperfect people being coached by other imperfect people. All of us have room for improvement. Even if you don't like what you hear, or you disagree, just listen and think about it. Try to learn more, even if you think it's unfair. People can and often do misinterpret our intentions. Information sharing can help put things back in synch. Above all, don't reject all feedback attributing it to gender or ethnicity. That tends to focus attention on something other than ourselves and prevents us from learning. Consider it to see if there is a kernel of truth before you reject it."

"Second, remember no matter how talented you are, attitude counts for a lot."

"There's a lot of discussion about attitude in your book, isn't there?"

"I hope so," said Jack. "People who shine have the type of attitude that attracts others. They know what's important, and they see themselves as part of the business, not as someone doing the job only for pay. Going the extra mile, being of service, smiling, being cheerful--all these behaviors attract others to us. I'm amazed when people allow themselves to be negative and arrogant. That pushes people away."

"I guess that includes what we talked about a long time ago. It's not about working harder or longer hours. It's about how you approach work. When you first told me that, I didn't get it. I do now, and it's made a big difference."

"There are many people working long and hard who aren't successful," said Jack, leaning forward in his chair. "You've got to think differently and build your capabilities."

"You've often told me to keep learning. I still am," said Rachel, turning to a fresh page in her pad. "What's third?"

"It's the golden rule of communication. If you want others to tune in, you have to be on their wave length. That means you may need to adjust your volume and alter your speed. Whether you're in a meeting or having a one-on-one conversation, if you want others to listen, don't shout. At the same time, don't speak so quietly that you can't be heard. You may need to change the speed too. If people look perplexed, you could be talking too fast. If they look bored, you could be talking too slow. There's a sound and a rhythm to organizational speech. If you can catch on to it, you add to the harmony. Listen to effective speakers and get some idea of why they are so effective. Also, watch your listener to get his or her response."

Rachel nodded. "I guess that's good advice for everyone. I sometimes talk too slow, and I need to watch that. Sometimes I've used more air time than I should. But don't listeners have an obligation too?"

"They do, but we both know there's a natural tendency for our minds to wander when we aren't fully engaged."

"That happens to me sometimes," said Rachel.

"I can take a hint," Jack laughed," so let's move on. Fourth, it's important to join with others, but don't give up being who you are in the name of being accepted. In an orchestra, the cello or the oboe is called on to solo because it has special qualities. Don't downplay yours. Next, if you have to choose between being loved and being respected, go for respect. Remember, love is freely given, but respect is earned. What I'm saying, Rachel, is this: I've seen people put up with offensive jokes or innuendoes and laugh along with everyone else just to gain the 'love' of the group. Every time you do this, you lower your self esteem, and you set yourself up for the next time. This doesn't encourage others to modify their behavior because they believe what they are saying doesn't bother you. If someone else finds the comment offensive, the person merely points to the fact that you thought it was funny too. At the same time, don't be like those who get offended at everything. That is downright childish, in my estimation."

"Mine too. I think whatever I choose, I need to let others understand who I am, don't you."

"So important. Finally, when things go well for you, don't abandon the others who could use a hand up. That's my list. I imagine others might have a different one." Glancing at his watch, Jack stood up. "Speaking of talking too much...."

Rachel knew the discussion was over. "I like your list, Jack. I think T.L. will too. Thanks for the advice. You talk about giving others a hand up. That's one thing I appreciate about you." With a smile, she was gone.

■ ■ ■

And Laura was gone too. She was off to the ballet with two close friends, leaving Jack on his own for the evening. Walking to the bookcase, he picked up a book about the rain forest. As he looked at the pictures, his thoughts drifted to his discussion with Rachel, to T.L., and to the beauty of the rain forest where over 3,000 different tree species thrive side by side. That was diversity! He put down the book and moving to his desk turned on the computer. It would be a long night.

The next morning Rachel found a brown envelope on her desk. It contained this note from Jack. "More on Chapter 11. Let me know what you think." She picked up the manuscript and read.

Jaro and I had spent the morning walking through the jungle with each of us pointing out the uses of particular berries, roots, plants, and fungi. I was delighted at his level of knowledge for I had thought the Panjus a more primitive people based on Koni and Jaro's appearance. I now understood what a mistake that was. Jaro had an inquisitive nature that he attributed to his culture. Just yesterday he had taught me a method developed by the Panjus for preparing ointments that was far superior to any I had ever seen. Jaro confessed that he too had drawn some assumptions based on the Korios "modern" dress. He had assumed that we had lost the old knowledge of medicines and was pleased to learn this wasn't so.

We stopped to rest and ate the sweet hog plum fruit we had picked earlier and wrapped in our bandannas. The silence was broken by the screech of a piha bird in the tree beside which Jaro was seated. We looked up. Spotlighted by narrow shafts of light, the tree was a circle of energy, alive with brightly-colored birds, tree frogs, and monkeys. Yet, I knew as tall as the the tree was, the part of its roots beneath the jungle floor were probably buried no deeper than the length of my arm. It was the lianas, huge vines that wrapped themselves around the tree on their climb toward the sun, that held it firmly to the ground. The fungi that lived on the tree roots nourished the tree. The insects of the jungle fed from the fungi, which helped feed the seeds of the beautiful flowers that lived atop the branches, creating beauty and drawing life from the tree. And the small animals of the jungle spread the life of the tree by dropping its seeds and fruit in new places.

The tree, with its strength and beauty, might appear to stand on its own, but without the various gifts brought to it by the lianas, the fungi, the birds, the animals, it would die. There was life in the jungle; there was death too, but the gifts that nourished the tree came from many different places--all varied, all beautiful, all one.

I looked over at Jaro and wondered if he had seen this too. He smiled and I knew.

JOURNAL ENTRY ELEVEN
To Survive: Treat everyone you work with as a worthy business partner.

To Succeed: Give helpful feedback to others and ask them to give you feedback as well.

To Shine: Invite and appreciate diversity. We all profit when we consider different perspectives and encourage free interchange of ideas.

The Twelfth Secret

On Discovering Your Purpose

"The purpose of life is not to be happy. It is to be useful, to be honorable, to be compassionate, to have it make some difference that you have lived and lived well."

– Ralph Waldo Emerson

Leaning back in his chair, his legs sprawled out in front of him, Jack clasped his hands behind his neck and yawned. He gazed out of the window watching the lights of the city just coming on. They sparkled against the evening sky. Winter! Thanksgiving was not too far off. And then....

"I know you're not busy," she said softly. She was standing in the doorway holding two steaming cups in one hand and her briefcase in the other.

"Come on in, Rachel," he laughed. "You caught me daydreaming."

"Look outside. It's more like night dreaming right now, Jack. I hate to disturb you, but I had to talk to you. I called Francine and she said you were still here. She gave me the tea. Said that you enjoy it at the end of the day."

"Francine is a jewel, and she knows that I can get my own."

"She told me you would complain. But I said, never mind him. Anyway, T. L. read the book and likes it a lot. He has made some notes on the things he found most useful, and we've been discussing some enabling ideas that will help him increase his network."

"That's great, but I sense there is more or you wouldn't be here at 6 o'clock. Paul making supper?"

"No, although he cooks more than I do. We're going out tonight. I know how busy you are, but I have a request from T.L., and I thought I should make it in person. Jack, he feels since you mentioned *purpose* in a number of places the book should provide some help in this direction. Know what I mean?"

"I think so. You're saying T.L. wonders how you know what your purpose is, right?"

"I guess that's it. To put a little meat around the bare bones, he's asking, 'How far do I want to go in my career, and how much am I prepared to sacrifice to get there?' I'd add to that some questions I've had from time to time, like how do you manage your business life so you still have a personal life? Is your work supplementary to your life or vice versa? Anyway, I promised I would bring it up to you. Now I have to go."

Jack stood up and put on his jacket. "Me too. I just need to put a few things away, and I'm out of here. Laura's got dinner on the stove, and she cooks a mean spaghetti. Rachel, I'm glad you stopped by. Those are good questions, and I'll give them serious thought. If you wanted to put me back to work on the book, you've succeeded. I've been away from *Secrets* too long. Time I finished it."

She picked up her briefcase. "Say hello to Laura."

"Enjoy your dinner. My best to Paul. I'll call."

The call came a week later. By then, the brown envelope had been delivered, opened, and read.

Keli's story continued....

Purpose
It was several years before I saw the Elder again. When he finally returned from his travels, he brought with him Yna, a Kupan woman he had taken

for a wife. We had rebuilt the village long before he returned, and thus they were able to stay in my hut while Manu, Barto, and I built a new dwelling to replace the one destroyed in the fire. In those first few weeks, there were few opportunities to talk alone. He was much in demand for all wanted to hear about the far off places he had been to and the strange things he had seen. Everyone in the village drew upon his wisdom and so some time went by before we climbed the hill together.

I was looking forward to our time alone for I knew we would have much to talk about, and yet with the passing of years, I sensed a difference in our relationship. He was still a father to me, but I was no longer a child. When we met early that morning, it was I who led the way and I who brought the cassavas and smoked capybara meat we would share. As we sat together once again enjoying the peacefulness of the hill, it was he that broke the silence.

"You have found your purpose, Keli."

"How did you know that?"

"Your eyes reveal your inner satisfaction and peace. That only comes when you have made your choice."

"Father, after you left, I spent some time with the Hunters. I traveled with Koni and the others through the deepest jungle to places where the only relief from darkness was the slender rays of sunlight that filtered through tree tops. It was a great adventure and I wanted to do it, but I came to understand it would not be my future. For several months I worked with Lutar and Tani helping them carve blowguns and bows from the spotted snakewood tree and make knives from peccary jaws. When the months had passed, I had renewed admiration for the Toolmakers, but I knew this was not the end of my search. I then went down the river with Manu, Kodi, and the other Traders. I enjoyed it a lot, but I was restless to return to the village. It was on this trip that I became fully aware of what I wanted to do and to be."

"And what was that, my son?"

"To stay a Healer, to teach and counsel others as you had taught and counseled me. I wanted to do these things, but I knew I wasn't ready. I needed to learn more about the mysteries of the jungle. How would I acquire

this knowledge? I could not draw upon your wisdom, for you were off on your travels. After some searching, I went to the Shaman and asked if he would allow me to learn under his teaching--to be his helper."

"That was a good solution. What was his answer?"

"He thought about it for nine days. On the tenth day, he asked me to walk with him."

"And?"

"He asked me how I had made this decision."

"And how did you?"

"It started on the day we met when I finally admitted to myself that I was lost. It took me some time to understand that experience for at the time I believed the most important thing in my life was to fit in. You helped me up and told me then that I needed to dedicate myself to learning if I wanted to find the path that leads to true contribution. What I came to understand is that path is different for everyone."

"That is true, my son, for each of us has his own gifts to share."

"Later when I was satisfied to stay in my role as a Sorter, you sensed my fear of losing my place in the tribe, and you encouraged me to move on. You told me I was on a journey, and you helped me see if I wanted to find my purpose I should listen to my thoughts, examine my heart, and be guided by what they told me."

"That's true, for no one can find a purpose for another."

"I thought many times about what was important to me, and I realized I was searching for something to give my life direction. My journey began when I got over my fears of not belonging. Thank you, Father, for helping me understand that. It continued as I struggled to find my own way when you left after the fire, and I realized my greatest satisfaction was in helping others. But even then, I wasn't sure. That is why I chose to walk through the jungle beside the Hunters, work with the Toolmakers, and travel with the Traders."

"Then you understood that following those paths was wrong for you."

"I did. But I also learned some other things. For when I walked with the Hunters, I discovered how greatly they valued my knowledge of medicines. I found myself advising them about various ointments and balms. To me, that was the best part of the hunt. The same was true when I worked with the Toolmakers and the Traders. My greatest satisfaction came from being of service. But how should I do that? Then I remembered something you told me."

"And that was?"

"You told me if I shot an arrow, I would know when it found its mark. So when I returned from my trading expedition, I spent some time thinking about exactly what I wanted. I had enjoyed being a Healer, but I did not want to go back to Sorting or Gathering."

"Aren't they all of service?"

"They are, but I wanted to do more, to learn more, to be more."

"When you spoke to the Shaman, were you aware of how much sacrifice might be required of you?"

"I was. And that was the conflict I had to resolve. I spoke to Mali about this. You may not know, Father, but she and I are promised."

"I guessed. I'm happy for you both. What did she tell you?"

"She will wait for me."

"How long will that be?"

"The Shaman tells me if he accepts me, it will be two years."

There were tears in the Elder's eyes. "He will accept you. We have spoken."

. . .

Jack smiled as he said good morning to Francine, but his heart wasn't in it. The old Packard had been acting up again and he was exasperated. "That's it!" he thought. "One more major repair job. If that doesn't do it, Laura and I will look at cars. No more roaming the street. The old boy will have to be satisfied spending the rest of his life on blocks in my garage."

With a piece of paper in her hand, Francine followed him into his office. "My goodness, you're in a hurry today. You walked by so fast I didn't have a chance to give this to you."

"Sorry," said Jack. "I've let the old crate make me late for the last time." He glanced at the sheet in his hand. It contained some bullet points with a note on the bottom. It read, "T.L put this together after reading Chapter 12. He describes it as the process for understanding one's purpose. He thought you might want to put it into your book if it makes sense. Francine says you have some time to talk at two thirty. See you then. Rachel. P.S. I invited T.L. to come along. Hope you don't mind."

Jack didn't mind at all. The morning would be filled with budget meetings. By two thirty he would welcome the time with T.L. and Rachel. Besides, he had something important to discuss with Rachel. He wondered how she would react to the news. Maybe this was the wrong time to talk about it. But when is the right time?

Jack was pacing when Rachel and T.L. knocked on the door. "Today's the day," he said aloud. Instantly he felt better as he walked to the door. As she came in with T.L., Rachel pretended to look around. "There must be someone hiding behind the drapes. I heard you talking." She grinned. "Things must be pretty bad when you're talking to yourself."

"I was, and they're not. Hi T.L. What did you bring this nosy lady up here for?" Everyone laughed. "I thought the bullet points captured the essence of the process T.L. and with your permission, I'll use it and credit you in the book."

T.L. smiled. "With pleasure. I like models. They help me focus. I'm still searching for my purpose, and I hope we can talk more about that today."

"You have the gist of it already," said Jack, looking once again at the bulleted points T.L. had given him.

FINDING PURPOSE

- Experience and Influence
- Reflection

- Exploration and Discovery
- Reflection
- Conflict Resolution
- Reflection
- Confirmation

"This is a map of Keli's journey to self-discovery," said Jack, "and mine as well. As you noted, it involves a process that alternates times of action with times of reflection. The journey can begin in many different ways--from a great personal hurt or success, key events, or perhaps from someone who inspires or influences us. The point is, we set out deliberately at some point to understand the meaning of these influences and experiences."

"So what you're saying is having these experiences is not enough. You have to take the time to think about the implications. Right?" asked T.L.

"That's vital. Otherwise you just go on to the next experience. That's how so many people live their lives, as part of a series of discreet activities and experiences. This is a road that can lead to ultimate dissatisfaction."

Rachel nodded. "That's why it was important in the story that Keli look for patterns that shaped his reactions to his time with the different groups. He must ask himself how, or if, they fit together. Where do the arrows hit?"

"Even then he should continue exploring, shouldn't he?" asked T.L. "When Keli joined the Hunters and the Traders he seemed to be testing his purpose to make sure he was making the right choice."

Jack nodded. "That's the way I see it."

"But what happens if you aren't sure, even after you have explored other things?" asked T.L.

"Keep exploring," answered Jack. "Some people never find their purpose because they don't take the time to look for it. Others are so eager to find their purpose that they stop too soon, and settle for something less than satisfying. Some people are totally influenced by others. They want to be just like dad or mom. They wind up trying to live someone else's dream and wind up disappointed or dissatisfied with their lives. The point is, something rings true for you. What is it? Each person must discover that for himself."

"Why can't someone else help you decide?" asked T.L. "There are important people in my life who want to be part of that decision. In my culture, we are devoted to our families."

"They are the influences that help to shape your experience. And they need to be considered and involved, so don't leave them out. What I'm really talking about is people who let others make these decisions or don't think about purpose at all. I see them as outer-directed. The problem is, being outer-directed fosters dependency and a continuous need for approval. That means others can control them, and that keeps them weak and powerless. To build enough confidence and self-esteem to handle the important decisions of life, you must be inner-directed. That means you are responsible and accountable for the decisions you make. If they are good ones for you, then you take credit. If they don't turn out that way, rather than blaming someone else, you accept the consequences and learn from them.

"Let's suppose," continued Jack, "you decide your purpose in life is to be the ideal son. That's up to you. What I'm suggested is, if that's your purpose, choose it wholeheartedly. Don't let someone else make that decision for you. In some sense, we make others pay when we make them responsible for our choices."

T.L. nodded. "That makes sense. I think I understand the process. What would help me is a real life example."

"I guess I'm elected," said Jack. "It's a long story, so let's start with the big picture. Over the years I've come to realize that each of us has our own special gifts. One of mine is the ability to explain abstract concepts in concrete ways using examples, metaphors, and stories. This gift has helped me explain the source of problems, come up with creative solutions, and generate enthusiastic support from others. Now I have three abiding interests in life. I enjoy people, business, and the outdoors. One of the values I've received from working at PWE is the opportunity to combine all three into a satisfying career.

"Over time I've come to realize my purpose: in order to succeed, people have to understand this business that is life and this life that is business. I see my purpose as helping with the latter."

"That's why you've been such a great mentor to me," interjected Rachel.

"I hope I've helped," said Jack smiling. "T.L. the model you drew explains the process. Of course, it's never quite as neat as that. Through scouting I developed a love for the outdoors--backpacking, camping, and fishing. When I was still a teenager I went rock climbing with a group in South America. I learned a lot about myself in those years. I learned to love and respect nature. I learned that I enjoyed working with others to overcome difficulties. In my last year of high school, I spent the summer doing volunteer work in a national forest. I got a lot of satisfaction contributing to something bigger than myself."

"I wonder why you didn't make your career in the outdoors," mused T.L.

"I was leaning in that direction," said Jack. " I took a year off from college travelling around and thinking about what I wanted to do with my life. Part of the time I spent in the rain forests of South America with my roommate, a biology major, who wanted to work for a pharmaceutical company doing research. As it turned out, he went to work for PWE. I wasn't interested in research. For me it was too analytical and removed from the excitement. When I returned from my trip, I spoke to the professor who was counseling me. He suggested that a career in marketing would give me the opportunity to travel, meet new people, be on the front lines. That sounded more like what I wanted, but he also told me if I wanted a career in a larger company with more opportunities, I needed an MBA, so I stayed in school."

"After graduating, I went to work for Reed and Connors, a competitor of PWE that specialized in brokering fruits. With R&C I thought I would be able to work with many different people, travel, and enjoy the outdoors too. I was mistaken. The first thing they did was put me in an office job with little interaction with people. It was then that I realized how much I missed working with and around people. Next they moved me into a retail grocery business, but there I spent my time dealing with a limited number of people and handling even more paperwork. I thought about my situation, but I didn't want to leave the company--not at first. Laura and I had married, and we were expecting our first child. That made job security important. I kept hearing how things would get better, but they didn't improve. R&C was a pretty closed company and even though I let my supervisor know I was dissatisfied, all I got back were platitudes and promises. Laura and I discussed this many times. Should I go for security or satisfaction? I decided I wanted both.

"That is why after seven years I left the company and went to work for Janek Markets, a small wholesale grocery chain operating mostly in third world countries. While there I traveled and saw many interesting parts of the world, but when I thought about it, I realized the most fulfilling part of the job was not the travel but mentoring younger employees. As for my interest in the outdoors, that was fulfilled on the weekends. Laura is a nature lover and we explored the outdoors together."

"So why did you leave Janek?" asked T.L.

"I didn't. It left me. Over time the company became highly profitable, and it was noticed by other companies, particularly R&C. When the merger began, I started looking around. My former roommate and good friend Dave Goldman was still happy at PWE. With his help and support I was hired into the Food Division where I developed my specialty in coffee. For a number of years I traded in the Andes, living part of my career here and part in that region of the world.

"During my time at PWE, I've had some positions I greatly enjoyed and others not as much--but even so, this is a great company. Four years ago, Hal Asher who was Senior Veep in charge of Human Relations offered me a promotion into HR. I was to start with the world's best project (at least in my eyes)--to set up a company-wide mentoring program under Human Relations' Bill Jameson. It was through that assignment that two things happened: first, I came to realize that mentoring is not a program but a relationship between two people, and second, it confirmed my earlier belief that what I loved most was helping people become successful. I also came to the conclusion that many people don't understand the way organizations work or how to be successful in today's world. Hence the book.

" So, T.L. if you thought that I started the book because I love writing, you'd be wrong. I started the book because I love to watch what happens when people get it. And, I used the metaphor of the jungle not only because I've been there, but because I love the mystery, the secrets, and most of all, the age-old wisdom it represents."

T.L. nodded. "I think that's a wonderful story, Jack. You should put it in your book."

Jack smiled. "Maybe the next one. This is Keli's story. With your model, people should be able to understand one of the most important concepts in it: we are most successful when we live out our purpose in life, not only in our personal lives but also in the hours we spend working."

T.L. turned to Rachel. "Have you found your purpose?"

"Yes," said Rachel. "it's taken me many experiences and a whole lot of introspection to be sure of what is important to me. Jack has played an essential role in this. What I want is to inspire others to take responsibility for their lives. That's why I see this concept of knowing what you want as so important."

"But how does your job enable you to do that?" asked T.L.

Rachel smiled. "It enables me to help others the way Jack helped me. Coaching and mentoring give me an opportunity to live my purpose. It's like passing on the joy of living to another person. In today's world, there are so many young people who want others to be responsible for their lives. They think life is supposed to be fun, and because of this they have a negative attitude toward work, which they see as drudgery rather than an opportunity to make a contribution and shine. Thus many of them miss the satisfaction and joy that comes from personal achievement. The more I think about it, the more sure I am of one thing--if I couldn't find true satisfaction in my work, it would be because I was living a life without purpose. Work, like education, is not about being entertained. Neither is it about expressing who you are. It's not just about taking selfies or telling your friends how you spent every day on social media. It's much more than that. And, it doesn't matter what work you do, either. When you shine, you taste the joy of living; and what's more, others notice it and opportunities come your way."

"That's one of the things I tried to bring out in Keli's story," said Jack. "Life is full of choices, all competing for our time and energy. The beauty of purpose is that it helps us resolve these conflicts, which, in turn, has a positive effect on our self-esteem and makes us better able to deal with larger problems."

"Well, Keli is fortunate," noted T.L. "Mali is willing to wait two years and to go along with his decision to study with the Shaman."

"True," replied Jack. "I suppose if she had refused, he would have to reconsider his purpose and determine what is most important to him. The key is, if he gives up his dream in order to make her happy, he may come to resent her. On the other hand, if he makes the choice to marry Mali now, he should enter into it gladly because making her happy will become the purpose of his life."

"Can't he do both?" asked T.L.

"Not in *Secrets*. He must make a choice. In the real world many people opt for both. It's often a continuous struggle of shifting priorities until they decide which takes precedence. When you can't decide, that's where negative stress comes from."

"I know you consider finding your purpose a key to the story," said T.L. "Could you tell me why--in a nutshell?"

"Well, I've already said that purpose helps us make choices," said Jack, "but there's more. It's what sets us apart. Look at the people who are most successful at PWE. They have a sense of what they believe and what they want. Purpose helps us gain the respect of others and increases confidence in our own judgment. It helps us manage our time and life better because we know what's important. There are so many things competing for our time today. Without purpose we can lose ourselves in a flurry of meaningless activities."

"Like I do sometimes when I wonder what happened to the day and what I accomplished," added Rachel. "If I stop then and refocus on what has meaning for me, I feel more in control."

"Right on!" added Jack. "I know people who put their total effort into their career for six months at a time and wonder why they don't have a life."

T.L. nodded in agreement. "I read a newspaper article once about a woman who said her goal at work was to keep busy. The reporter thought that was great."

Rachel laughed. "Busy doing what? I feel sorry for anyone who is totally activity driven."

"And outer-directed," added Jack.

"And speaking of busy, we've taken enough of your time Jack. But if you can spare it, I need a minute or two alone with you."

T.L. and Jack shook hands as Jack ushered him out and closed the door. "What's up?"

"Jack, I'm excited. Do I have news for you!"

"I have news too. You go first."

"I've been promoted. It won't be announced till next week, but I'm moving into Human Resources University and College Recruiting. I have so many plans, so many things I'd like to go over with you."

"Congratulations," he said. "I'm proud of you."

"I guess I'm kind of like Keli. I look back and see all the things you've done for me, and...."

"Now don't get teary on me," said Jack, swallowing hard. "I have some news too. I'm taking early retirement from PWE, Rachel. I'll be leaving the end of next month."

The tears. He could see them welling up in her eyes. "How will I ever get along without you, Jack. You've been like...."

"Don't you dare say 'like a father to me,'" he smiled. "And don't cry or I'll cry too."

There was a long silence during which Rachel fiddled with her notebook. Then she looked up. "What brought this on? What will you do?"

"Writing the chapter on purpose helped. I've been pulled so many ways. I want to write, but I've been so busy. Now I've got a publisher, and...."

She broke out in a wide smile. "Whoopee. You're going on a book tour, aren't you?"

"Something like that. I'll be doing some media among other things. Laura and I will have more time to spend together, and I will, of course, keep in touch." He walked to his desk and from behind it brought out a box, gift wrapped, with a red ribbon on top. "Here, Rachel. I want you to have this."

"But what's the occasion," she asked.

"Call it a celebration gift. When I saw this at the store, I thought of you. You're highly thought of at PWE, and the future looks good. I'm very proud of you."

"Jack, this isn't fair. It is I who should be giving you a gift. You're the one who's leaving."

"If you want to give me a gift, promise me this...that you will pass on the secrets I have shared with you to others who long for success and aren't sure of the way. There are many out there, and all they need is someone like you to point them in the right direction."

"I promise."

"And Rachel, do remember how important Paul is in your life. Carve out more time for him. It pays big dividends."

"Always my teacher."

"Always your friend."

It was later that week when Rachel put the next entry in her journal.

JOURNAL ENTRY 12

To Survive: Know your purpose and use it to set priorities and to make choices in your life.

To Succeed: Make sure your work relates to your purpose and makes a difference in your organization.

To Shine: Remember this--being inner-directed makes you better able to unravel the mysteries of the jungle for yourself and others.

Epilogue: On Becoming a Mentor

"A teacher affects eternity; he can never tell where his influence stops."

Henry Brooks Adams

Dear Jack,

I'm speechless. What a wonderful surprise to come to my office today and find a package from you sitting in the middle of my desk. The book looks wonderful. I mean, after reading the manuscript, it is so exciting to see a real book waiting for me--and a letter from you to boot. You've made my day. Are you planning a sequel? I know Keli will complete his education with the Shaman and marry Mali, so I guess his future is set. Still, I am sure there are so many other stories you could tell about the organizational jungle.

It sounds like you have had great fun publicizing your book. So now, you're off to the Greek Islands on vacation. How I envy you. But I'm happy for you and Laura. In answer to your question, yes I am holding up my end of PWE just fine though I miss our long talks. It's hard to believe it has been almost a year since you left. And yes, I am keeping my promise. How could I not?

Do you remember Marsha Nichols? She's the young accountant who works for Dan Chambers, the tax attorney down the hall from me. Dan's pretty gruff, but he has the legendary heart of gold. I had gotten the impression that he was not all that happy with Marsha, but I suspected it was more a personality conflict than a performance issue. Anyway, one day a few months ago I was sitting in my office working on an agenda for a meeting when I heard loud voices in the hall close to my office. (You don't know how many times I have regretted having an office close to the coffee room.) Anyway, I got up to close the door just in time to see Marsha hurrying away. Billie Washington, Dan's paralegal, was standing there, hands on hips.

"Excuse the commotion, Rachel," she said. "I know we must have disturbed you. I just can't take that woman. She's got a problem with her mouth and a chip on her shoulder that's too big for me to knock off. No wonder she eats lunch alone." Billie always did have a gift for words.

I told Billie I was sorry she and Marsha were having problems, and, mumbling a couple of other pat phrases, managed to shut the door before she could say much more. When Billie feels offended, she can go on and on, if you know what I mean. Anyway, a few minutes later I heard a tap on my door--just one tap, mind you. When I opened it, there was no one there, but I saw Marsha walking toward the coffee room. Now I remembered that you had a role in recruiting her and thought a lot of her, and I was curious about what she might have wanted, so I grabbed my cup and followed her in there to see if I could find out. I really wasn't sure how she would react if I asked her why she had knocked once and walked away. Marsha has built quite a reputation. In the year she has been on our floor she has become known as an aggressive, combative loner. But there in the coffee room she didn't look like she wanted to fight. In fact, I recognized the same lost expression on her face you must have seen from across your desk when you looked at mine several years ago. "Marsha, was that you at my door?" I asked her.

She blushed. "Yes, but I decided not to disturb you."

I told her I was taking a break for some coffee and invited her to my office. For a short time we sat across the desk and looked at each other in silence. Finally, Marsha spoke. "You're a friend of Jack's, aren't you?"

"A good friend," I told her.

"He's always been such a nice man. I'm sorry he left. If you hear from him, please tell him I said hello." I nodded, and she started to leave, but I had a feeling she had not said what was on her mind.

"Don't go yet, Marsha," I said. "Tell me how things are going for you."

She sighed and sank down in a chair. "Not well. I guess you heard the noise in the hall. You would have had to be unconscious not to. Billie and I were going at it again. At least we speak. That's more than I get from most people around here--except you. You've been friendly from the first and I appreciate it. Anyway, I'm sorry we disturbed you. That's what I came to say."

"I'm sorry things aren't going well for you, Marsha. Jack used to sing your praises. He said you were intelligent, articulate, and a real leader in school. That's why PWE worked so hard to recruit you."

"Really. I wish he'd have told that to Dan. I get the impression he doesn't see it that way."

"I'm sorry," I told her. "I know how hard it is to work when you don't feel appreciated. How long have you been here?"

"At PWE, almost three years. Working for Dan, eleven months. Ask me how long I'm staying. That's probably a better question."

"And what would you answer?"

"I'm not sure. I don't even know why I said that. I'm just not happy. Most people are so unfriendly. It's like everyone else is playing off one sheet of music and I'm playing off another. "

Jack, in that moment I wondered how many lost souls roam our halls and the halls of other organizations. And I understand now why you asked me to make that promise. You've left me to carry on what you started, haven't you. That's fine because you helped me so much that I really want to pass it on to others. That day I told Marsha a story -- about torches and lamps--and me. I've been mentoring her the past two months using your manuscript because I didn't have the book. We're up to Chapter Five. Now that it's out, I'm going to get five more copies--one for Marsha and the rest to give away. Of course, I won't part with mine because it's a gift from you, but they should be here in a couple of days. There are other Marsha's and Keli's who can profit from your wisdom. Of that, I am sure. What I never realized before you was how much satisfaction there is in helping another person. I think you can tell, I'm hooked.

But, Jack, you know me. I like to be thorough, like you. So I decided if I was going to become half the mentor you are, I would need to be sure I had the qualities it takes. I have made a list of them based on watching you in action. I'd love to know what you'd add to the list, but here are my seven in no particular order.

One thing a mentor needs is a genuine interest in others. I know people who never smile, never take a moment to say hello. You meet them in the hall, and they ask you how you are feeling and keep on walking. They seem too preoccupied to care. People like that don't know what they're missing. From the first, I felt you cared about me. I knew you were someone I could confide in, someone who would really listen without making me feel foolish, and I was sure you sincerely wanted to help.

The second quality is empathy. It's one thing to care but to truly understand how another feels, that's special. I was the one with the problems, but you had a way of accepting my feelings, of seeing the world from my point of view. I knew you didn't always agree with me, and that was helpful too. Whether I was furious about my performance appraisal or confused about moving into the marketing job, I felt understood.

Third is perspective. How easy it is to lose our sense of proportion when faced with a problem. I know I did. It was your gift to help me look beyond the immediate moment and even past my own interests to broader issues. I remember when we talked about the five levels of commitment, and I realized how stuck I was in my own world. You made me realize I was Rachel, Inc., and part of a larger enterprise. I asked you then which level of commitment you identified with me, but you had the wisdom and objectivity to let me be the judge. That was powerful, and it's one quality I'm going to work hard to emulate. You taught me that good mentors share their perspectives, but they don't make judgments.

Fourth is balance. I'm sure I would have preferred at times that you totally agree with me, but you helped me see situations from both sides. Was I overreacting? Was there a lesson for me? Only a true friend can do that. I can tell you first hand, it's easy to fall into the trap of becoming an advocate, but that doesn't help the other person. Balance is a particular challenge for me with Marsha. She's had a couple of challenging supervisors, and it's a continuing struggle to help her understand how much her defensiveness contributes to her problems. She's coming around though. She's been getting some praise from Dan lately, and she and Billie have actually started going to lunch. I think I see some daylight.

Fifth is the willingness to openly admit our own mistakes. When I came to you with problems, it helped me a lot when you let me know you had been there. I probably would not have been as willing a learner if you had preached from a lofty pedestal. But you never did, Jack. One of the rules for mentors, I think, is to share our own struggles. When I got that mediocre performance review from Bill, I was devastated. What helped me most is when you told me of a similar situation from your past. I thought, "If Jack overcame this, so can I."

Because you were successful, I had confidence in your advice. That is the sixth quality and an essential one. I guess you can call it credibility. Once I asked you if mentors were really necessary. I remember the golf analogy you used. "If you want to learn the game, you can hit a thousand balls at the driving range or you can take lessons from a pro." You're a pro, and if I hadn't seen you that way, I would not have placed such a high value on your counsel. I think that's important for anyone who relies on another for advice. Apparently, Marsha sees me that way. I only hope I'm worthy of her trust.

Finally, a good mentor musts have a sense of humor. So much of what goes on in organizations is deadly serious. Whether it's being in the midst of a downsizing or struggling through turf problems, you have to help people see the lighter side. Why? Because unless you can laugh at your own mistakes, it's hard to find creative solutions. Remember when Bill told me to "lighten up"? I really think I did, thanks to you. You have a way of putting things in perspective--of seeing the humor in situations and helping me see it too.

So there's my list. I may think of more later on, but if I get these down, I'll have it made. I keep the list in my lap drawer, and I'm working to improve in all areas.

Now, let me respond to your other questions. First of all, T.L. is doing great. He's moved on to Treasury, where his analytical skills and expertise in foreign exchange have Mel Ashton grinning from ear to ear. Even though I'm no longer in the group, we stay in touch. I was invited to his going away party. He chose the restaurant--Alfredo's. I believe that's one of your favorite restaurants too. We all spent the evening eating pasta and listening to Italian tenors sing opera. What a fun night that was!

Oh, and you asked for a copy of my journal, so here it is. The original sits on the small table in my office next to your lovely gift.

Thank you for being the most wonderful mentor anyone could ever have. I know you're awfully busy with the book and all, but Paul and I would love to have you and Laura come to dinner when you get back home. Please give us a call.

Hugs to Laura,
Rachel

Carefully she folded the letter and sealed the envelope containing it and her journal, placing it on the table next to the beautiful crystal lamp Jack had given her the day he told her he was leaving. Rachel had kept it and the journal in her office as a constant reminder of her promise. She picked up *Secrets* admiring the cover, a simple drawing of an ocelot sitting on a branch, its head half hidden by leaves. Just like the mysteries of the jungle, she thought. She opened the book for the first time and smiled. Then her eyes filled with tears. There would be one last journal entry after all.

RACHEL'S JOURNAL

Beneath the heading, she copied the dedication from *Secrets of the Jungle*:

"To Rachel, a lamp whose light radiates wherever she goes. Here is the greatest secret. Remember it, and share it with others: If you would be successful, think of all the things you prize and willingly bestow them on another. If you want trust, trust others; if you want credit, give it to others; if you want praise, praise others; if you want love, then love others. Yours is the legacy of the lamp. Keep shining. Your friend, Jack."

References

Forsyth, Adrian and Ken Miyata. *Tropical Nature: Life and Death in the Rain Forests of Central and South America.* New York: Macmillan, 1984.

Loden, Marily and Judy B. Rosener. *Workforce America: Managing Employee Diversity as a Vital Resource.* Donnelley, 1991.

Mager, Robert F. and Peter Pipe. *Analyzing Performance Problems or You Really Oughta Wanna.* Atlanta, Georgia: CEP Press, 1997.

Nowak, Ronald M. Walkers. *Mammals of the World,* Vol. II. Baltimore and London: John Hopkins University Press, 1991.

Plotkin, Mark J. *Tales of a Shaman's Apprentice.* New York: Viking, 1993.

Thomas, R. Roosevelt, Jr. with Tracy Irving Gray, Jr. and Marjorie Woodruff. *Differences Do Make a Difference.* Atlanta, Georgia: American Institute for Managing Diversity, 1992.

Wassman, Thomas and Hans Joseph Frohlich; et al. *The Plight of the Tropical Rainforest: Vanishing Eden,* editor North American Edition: Edward G. Atkins, Ph.D. Hauppage, New York: Barron's Educational Series, 1991.

Other Books by Shirley Peddy

The Art of Mentoring: Lead, Follow and Get Out of the Way
This book covers some of the more contentious mentoring issues in organizations today: helping the new employee master the work and unspoken rules, improving interpersonal skills, dealing with job dissatisfaction, workaholism, cynicism, and the lack of motivation" (preface). It shows how to foster a mentoring culture in which people are rewarded for helping each other succeed. As one reader wrote, "Although an easy read because of her story telling style, Peddy provides her readers with hard-won insights into the culture of organizations and the role of mentoring relationships in this age of disposable employees."

These insights come through the story of Rachel Hanson, an organizational consultant for Perry Winkle Enterprises (PWE), sent as temporary marketing manager to To Your Health (TYH) a recently acquired subsidiary whose sales have been dropping. Her assignment is to assess the reasons for the decline, see if it can be turned around, and decide which of the five marketers should be retained and which terminated or reassigned. She decides to focus on mentoring as a potential solution for all. However, it is not as easy as it sounds. As a temporary manager, she encounters a variety of problems in an atmosphere in which employees feel unappreciated by management, threatened by the takeover, hostile, and even indifferent. Through this story line the reader will discover the four purposes of mentoring, the process of redesigning a job, how to deal with difficult employees, when and how to use straight talk, how to counsel, advise, and help another succeed, as well as ten principles that every mentor should practice and ten that every person being mentored needs to remember.

Booklist calls it, " Thoughtful...accessible...entertaining." Still, another reader says it is a "must read" for leaders in his organization.

The Lady Killers: A Thriller **by Shirley (Peddy) Eads, PhD and Professor Jody C. Heymann**

When a popular Texas State Senator running for reelection hires an assassin to solve his problem with a young lover threatening to expose him, he gets more than he bargained for: a murderer who enjoys his work, a media eager to exploit any scandal, and two sister detectives, hired by the coed's parents to find their missing daughter. The Senator is one of the lady killers. The other is known as The Shark because of the cold-blooded way he takes out anyone who might get too close to uncovering his identity.

While the local media zeroes in on a potential scandal, the sisters split up the investigation which moves from Victoria's college and the disappearance of a potential witness to the other women who know the Senator intimately. When the sisters get too close to the truth, they become the Shark's next quarry.

EXCERPT:
"The wind, howling through the fireplace, filled the house with an eerie noise. Kate decided to go downstairs and turn on the security system. She stood at the top of the landing glancing downward. The bottom floor was dark with only a small bit of illumination from the night light on the stairs. Was that the shadow of a figure moving quickly away or a tree limb waving and visible through the glass pane in the door? There were light switches at both the top and bottom of the stairway, but she was hesitant to turn them on. What if someone was inside? What if he was waiting for her at the bottom of the stairs? No, it would be best to go back to the desk and get her Smith. Then she could turn the light on and move quickly aside to avoid who knows what. She kicked off her shoes and backed up to the desk.

"Without turning around, she reached in and slowly pulled out the revolver. Swiftly she returned to the landing. Mentally counting to three, Kate switched on the light at the top of the staircase and moved to her left. Everything was still. As she stepped down the stairs, she heard a strange nose as if someone were turning a key in the lock. She called out, "Allison, is that you?" knowing it was not her sister but hoping to alarm anyone who might try to gain access to the house....

"He was standing near the window, beside the shrubs on the right side of the house. The hurricane shutters were up, and the drawn shades gave her a false sense of security. Surprise would have been on his side, that is, if he had decided to grab her tonight. He chuckled as he played with the five cartridges in his pocket. She thought that the gun would help her but not if it wasn't loaded. He had been in the house again tonight, then changed his mind and decided to wait. He wanted both of them. Thanks to Mel Grant he knew they had his name.... So why was he hanging around? He liked watching her, and even more, he loved the sense of fear in her. She was like a puppet. He made a little noise like putting the master key in her lock and she ran around with her unloaded revolver trying to find out what was going on. He laughed to himself. He loved playing cat and mouse with her. He hadn't had this much fun with a woman for a long time."

The Author

Shirley Peddy (Eads) is author of *The Art of Mentoring* (1999), *Secrets of the Jungle* (1996), *The Lady Killers: A Thriller*, co-authored by Jody C. Heymann, (2015) and *Shine: Winning at Work* (2017). An award-winning trainer and training designer, Dr. Peddy has addressed numerous conferences all over the United States and in foreign countries. She is a recognized authority on mentoring.

Her organizational knowledge is grounded in almost twenty years of experience as an internal consultant and leader of a training organization for a major oil company where she consulted with an advisory committee of executives and managers. Her communication background includes being on the faculty of Louisiana State University, where she taught honors English, serving as Chairperson of the English Department at Dominican College in Houston, and teaching as an Associate Professor of English at Del Mar College in Corpus Christi, Texas.

Peddy's educational background includes a B.S. degree in Education from The University of Texas, an M.A. degree in English from University of Houston, a Ph.D. from Louisiana State University and professional certification in Organizational Development from National Training Labs.

Dr. Peddy's work is dedicated (1) to helping people achieve power over their lives and satisfaction in their work and (2) encouraging organizations to help people succeed by rejecting the idea that employees are disposable in favor of a culture that rewards mentoring.

Now semi-retired from her consulting and educational careers, Shirley Peddy lives in Corpus Christi, Texas. She looks back on her years with an international company, where she enjoyed a productive and rewarding career, as a learning experience that she should share with those who are motivated to seek the rewards and opportunities that come from "winning at work."

www.ingramcontent.com/pod-product-compliance
Lightning Source LLC
Chambersburg PA
CBHW030744180526
45163CB00003B/916